BIOFEEDBACK

 MAYFIELD PUBLISHING COMPANY

BIOFEEDBACK
AN INTRODUCTION
AND GUIDE

David G. Danskin
Kansas State University

Mark A. Crow
St. John's Hospital
Salina, Kansas

Dorothy and Robin gave us spirit
Pete gave us space
Lisa made it look right
Jain brought velocity

Library of Congress Catalog Card Number: 80-84020
International Standard Book Number: 0-87484-530-0

Manufactured in the United States of America
Mayfield Publishing Company
1240 Villa Street
Mountain View, CA 94041

Compositor: HMS Typography
Printer and binder: George Banta Company
Sponsoring editor: Robert W. Erhart
Managing editor: Liz Currie
Manuscript editor: Tom Belina
Designer: Nancy Sears
Illustrator: Mary Burkhardt
Production: Michelle Hogan

CONTENTS

FOREWORD   ix

PREFACE   xi

1   **BIOFEEDBACK: WHAT AND WHY**   1

2   **STRESS**   5

The Germ Theory   7
The High Cost of Stress   8
The Physiology of Stress   9
Personality and Stress   15
Selye's General Adaptation Syndrome   17
Our Perceptions Talk   19

3   **ST: SKIN TEMPERATURE
BIOFEEDBACK TRAINING**   22

Autogenic Training and ST Feedback   22
    Migraine Headaches   24
    Raynaud's Disease   25
    Hypertension   26

Other Applications of ST   28
Instruments for ST Biofeedback Training   29
Initial Hook-Up and Training   32
    Self-Directing Phrases and Visualizations   34
    Discovering Internal States   35

4 EMG: MUSCLE TENSION BIOFEEDBACK TRAINING   38

How EMG Training Works   38
Initial Hook-Up and Training   40
Relaxation Training Techniques for EMG   41
Specific Applications of EMG   42
    Tension Headache   43
    Anxiety   45
    Phobias   47
    Psychosis   47
Other Applications of EMG   48

5 EEG: BRAIN WAVE BIOFEEDBACK TRAINING   52

Brain Wave Rhythms   53
    Beta Rhythm   55
    Alpha Rhythm   55
    Theta Rhythm   55
    Delta Rhythm   55
Instruments for EEG Training   56
Wiring Up and Training   56
The Heritage of EEG   58
Applications of EEG for Behavioral and Physical
    Disorders   61
Applications of EEG for Creativity and Learning   63
The Future of EEG Biofeedback   65

6 OTHER FORMS OF BIOFEEDBACK TRAINING   68

Galvanic Skin Response   68
Heart Rate Feedback   70
Blood Pressure Feedback   71
Experimental Forms of Biofeedback   72
    Stethoscope Feedback   72

Respiration Feedback   73
Vapor Pressure Feedback   74
Stomach Acidity Level Feedback   75
Sphincter Feedback   75
Stabilimeter Feedback   75
Blood Chemistry Level Feedback   76

7 SELECTING BIOFEEDBACK CENTERS
   AND TRAINING   78
Locating a Biofeedback Training Center   78
Qualifications   79
Some Cautions   81
    Medical Considerations   81
    Inaccurate Instruments   81
    Psychological Considerations   82

8 BIOFEEDBACK TRAINING IN EDUCATION   83
Remediation   84
    Reading Problems   84
    Speech Anxiety   85
    Test Anxiety   85
    Hyperactivity   86
    Learning Disabilities   87
    Stuttering   88
Prevention and Development   89
    Research with Armed Forces Personnel   90
    Loretta Engelhardt's Biofeedback and Relaxation
        Skills Program   90
    Norma Estrada and Student Training   91
    Counseling Center, Kansas State University   92
    Speaking Behavior   93
    Biofeedback and Computer-Assisted
        Instruction   93
    Learning and Recall   93
    Children, Parents, and Self-Regulation   94
Biofeedback in Education   94

⑨ **RELAXATION TECHNIQUES** 98
Tense–Relax 99
Autogenic Training 101
Visualization 102
Self-Directed Imagery 102
Breathing 103
The Waiting Game (Mini-Exercises) 104

ADDITIONAL READING AND LISTENING 107

GLOSSARY 109

INDEX 113

FOREWORD

During the past decade, interest in self-directed health behavior and programs grew at an amazing rate. Biofeedback—and its implications for a higher level of wellness and an improved quality of life—moved out of the laboratory and became available to an ever-increasing number of people. It soon became evident that there was a strong need for reliable information from health educators, mental health professionals, and research scientists about biofeedback.

Biofeedback: An Introduction and Guide is a readable, no-nonsense examination of biofeedback and its uses. The authors provide practical and realistic information on the clinical, counseling, medical, and educational uses of biofeedback training. The book should appeal to anyone in classrooms, seminars, or workshops who wants reliable information regarding biofeedback and self-regulation.

It is noteworthy that biofeedback training requires the individual to take responsibility for his or her own progress. Here, as in many areas of American health care, the "patient" has become a "client"—not a passive recipient of prescribed services, but a person who knows what he wants and takes an active role in the treatment or training process. Clinically and educationally, it is gratifying to work with people in this manner, and impressive to see them develop more self-responsibility and increased self-regulation.

Are we health professionals ready and able to meet the challenge from our constituency—the people to whom we provide health services? I personally hope so. One way to meet this challenge is to better inform them of ways in which they can more effectively help themselves. This book should help promote better public understanding, develop greater public support, and facilitate increased public use of biofeedback.

The Menninger Foundation   E. Dale Walters
                                              Director of Educational Services
                                                and Programs
                                              Voluntary Controls Program

PREFACE

Biofeedback: An Introduction and Guide is a concise, practical examination of the techniques and uses of biofeedback training. The instructor of workshops or seminars as well as the individual seeking ways to become more actively involved in maintaining his or her own health will find it a simple yet complete map to one of the most rapidly expanding self-directed programs in the health care field.

Biofeedback begins with a discussion of basic questions—what is biofeedback and how does it work—and then examines the causes and results of stress in human life. With this foundation laid, the text then describes the various forms of biofeedback training, using skin temperature, muscle tension, brain waves, and other body responses. How to choose a biofeedback center and some cautions about the field are presented next, followed by a discussion of the uses of biofeedback in education. A set of relaxation techniques and exercises concludes the book. A glossary of technical terms is provided at the back of the text.

In an emerging field such as biofeedback, the comments and suggestions of individuals actively involved in training and research are especially important. We would like in particular to thank Alan Brauer, Stress Reduction and Biofeedback Medical Center; Patricia Hodges, California State University, Los Angeles; Ralph Mann, University of Kentucky; Douglas W. Matheson, College of the Pacific; and Gary E. Schwartz, Yale University, for their perceptive critiques of our manuscript.

1

BIOFEEDBACK:
WHAT AND WHY

What is biofeedback? And why should you need to know about it? Consider the following real life situations:

A disc jockey has had insomnia for months. His sleeplessness begins to interfere with his job. When his radio hours are switched from afternoon to morning, his insomnia increases. He becomes panicky and his work suffers even more. After biofeedback training he can usually fall asleep at will within five minutes upon going to bed at night.

A young mother is frustrated and angry over her infant's frequent crying; her temper wears thinner by the day. After biofeedback training she finds she can cope more patiently and lovingly with her child. She becomes more relaxed and loses her temper less often.

A college student has trouble concentrating when trying to study for an exam. She thumbs through the pages of her books and daydreams. When a friend interrupts her, she responds immediately, as if relieved to turn away from the task in front of her. When she returns to her books, her mind wanders to thoughts of Christmas vacation and what she has planned for all that free time. In two hours she actually studies for only about fifteen minutes. After biofeedback training, she is not easily interrupted in her study when friends stop by, and daydreams do not distract her. She can concentrate steadily for an hour, and a short break is all she needs to refresh herself before she tackles her next subject.

A lawyer is diagnosed as having high blood pressure. He applies for additional life insurance and is told that because of his blood pressure he must pay higher premiums. His doctor also tells him that he may need to start taking regular medication—a costly and usually lifelong procedure. Two months later, after biofeedback training, his blood pressure reading has dropped to within the normal range, and his doctor says that he needs no medication. His insurance policy is issued at the standard rate.

We could offer many other examples: the student who was once terrified about speaking before the class but now remains calm and collected; the homemaker whose phobia made her tremble at the thought of shopping in crowded stores but can now shop freely anywhere she chooses; or the teenager who once felt so uncomfortable about socializing with his peers that he drank a six-pack of beer every Friday and Saturday night but can now feel relaxed and accepted while remaining sober.

We have seen each of these cases in our own work and in each case the individual used skills learned from biofeedback training to treat his or her own difficulties.

Much has been written about the "healing capability" of biofeedback. The claims and counterclaims about its effectiveness have resulted in confusion among practitioners as well as the general public. What can be said with certainty is this: biofeedback is a scientifically-based, self-therapeutic technique that has proved successful when used by people suffering from a variety of illnesses and disorders. *As with any technique, however, there is no guarantee that biofeedback will bring about improvement of a specific disorder. Just as prescribed medication may have different effects on different people, any one type of biofeedback training may be helpful for many persons, but no one form of treatment will be "right" for everyone.*

This book attempts to give thorough but uncomplicated answers to the questions that we in the field are most often asked by individuals who are starting or considering biofeedback training. What is biofeedback? For whom does it work? How do you do it? What kinds of health problems are most effectively relieved by this form of treatment? Is it of any value for "healthy" people? And many others.

Let us return to our opening question, What is Biofeedback? The complete answer requires three definitions: one for *biofeedback,* a second for *biofeedback training,* and a third for *voluntary self-regulation.* Let us examine these one at a time.

What is *biofeedback?* The simplest definition is this: it is information about an individual's biological functions. Actually, each of us has been receiving some information of this sort all our lives. For example, every time you use a simple bathroom scale you get direct feedback on your own weight control. When you think you may have a fever and put a thermometer in your mouth, the thermometer reading (the biological feedback) tells you something about what is going on inside you. When you count your pulse before, during, and after jogging, you get feedback about your physiological reactions, which can help you "see" the effects that jogging has on your body. And how about the doctor's blood pressure cuff or stethoscope? If you were to read the blood pressure meter or listen to your heartbeat through a stethoscope, you would receive the same biological feedback as the doctor.

Note that none of the instruments does anything *to* you. The scale, the thermometer, the jogger's fingers for feeling a pulse, the blood pressure cuff, and the stethoscope only give you information about something inside you. Each instrument acts as an external mirror for your internal states. Simply stated, this is biofeedback.

The explosion in technology since World War II has produced sensitive instruments that respond to very slight changes in the body, and these have made possible the growth of biofeedback. Before these were developed, the instruments available for measuring minute changes in biological functions were bulky, expensive, and unreliable. The new developments in electronics have produced portable and extremely reliable equipment capable of feeding back—by meters, sounds, or lights—changes in temperature as small as one-tenth to one-hundredth of a degree, or changes of just one or two beats per minute in the heart rate, or very small blood pressure changes and minute changes in muscle tension. Thus, today you can watch a meter and see the constant changes in tension in one of your muscles, or changes in the rate of your heartbeat, or changes in your blood pressure. These instruments usually run on batteries, and cannot shock or "invade" a person's body; safety of use is emphasized in their design and manufacture. It is the biofeedback gained from such instruments that we are concerned with in this book.

Biofeedback training is using instrument feedback to learn how to make changes *voluntarily* in whichever process is being monitored. By watching an instrument give continuous measurements of a body function, a person can experiment with different thoughts, feelings, and sensations and get immediate feedback on their physical effects. For example, what thoughts result in increased heart rate? What thoughts result in decreased heart rate? With practice, and with the information provided by the sensitive biofeedback instrument, the trainee can learn to alter heart rate, or change the level of muscle tension, or learn to lower blood pressure, or even to increase skin temperature in parts of the body. This is biofeedback training.

Voluntary self-regulation—the goal of biofeedback training—is the ability to achieve the bodily changes without the feedback instrument. By practicing with instruments, one can gain increased awareness and sensitivity to internal sensations. Later, after dedicated and continued practice, these internal cues can be recognized without the aid of an instrument. Then, the skill of voluntarily regulating a bodily change—for example, decreasing blood pressure or heart rate—can be integrated into a person's daily life.

Three things are essential in achieving voluntary self-regulation. The first is getting immediate, accurate, and continuing feedback of internal biological processes; this is what biofeedback instruments provide. The second is training—learning what the feedback means. The third is being able to apply what you learn in biofeedback training to your daily life—in other words, learning how to integrate this new knowledge so that it becomes a natural part of you.

Biofeedback training, then, is like learning to play tennis or golf or badminton. In these sports, a person practices a shot and gets immediate feedback—an observable result. With this feedback, changes can be made so that the desired skill is finally achieved. It takes practice and more practice to master the basic strokes in tennis. The same is true of biofeedback training.

Biofeedback training differs from conventional medical treatment. In traditional treatments, an individual is inoculated to protect against germs causing disease, or is given some form of medication to treat the disease, or undergoes surgery to repair or remove damaged tissue. The individual is passive, while the drugs or the surgery do the work.

With biofeedback, the person takes a more active role in the treatment by training and learning how to voluntarily regulate the bodily function that is causing the problem. The person is, to a degree, both the patient and the doctor. Although the role of the biofeedback trainer is initially an important one, the individual taking the training has much more of a central role in his or her own treatment than is often the case in traditional medicine. The individual accepts responsibility for his own improvement We should stress, however, that *biofeedback training as a treatment for a medical problem should not be engaged in without seeing your physician first.* We require this in the trainings we conduct, as do all competent biofeedback therapists.

At present, the focus in most biofeedback training is on helping persons solve medically related problems on their own. Its future may well lie in helping to prevent many of these problems as well as to help individuals learn to enhance normal levels of mental and physical performance. Because biofeedback is a relatively new field, as was laser technology a few years ago, future applications in other areas are as yet unproven or unknown.

It is known, however, that biofeedback can be especially effective in helping people learn to control stress. Before we explore biofeedback techniques and applications, let us first take a close look at the general problem of stress in contemporary American society. Helping individuals handle stress is the focus of most biofeedback training today.

2

████████████████████

STRESS

For the past several years, the American public has been inundated with articles, books, and special reports about stress. Nearly every day some doctor, researcher, or institution releases new information linking stress to one disease or another. Why this preoccupation with stress? The main reason is that diseases associated with stress have been reported to be the leading causes of death in the United States today. In the twentieth century, the percentage of deaths caused by just heart attacks and strokes (both related to stress) has increased 300 percent and claims more lives in the United States than all other causes of death combined. The American Heart Association estimates that 4,240,000 persons have coronary heart disease and another 1,820,000 have had strokes.[1]

Stress is not the only factor implicated in the increase of these diseases. Other factors seem to be genetic disposition, diet, exercise patterns, environmental influences, and consumption of alcohol and tobacco. However, some of these factors—such as drinking and smoking—are now understood to be attempts used by some individuals to handle stress, and thus are stress-aided factors.

Millions more are suffering from diseases and disorders closely linked to stress. Over 34 million have hypertension (high blood pressure).[2] Stress may possibly be the major factor in hypertension. How this could be so will be discussed later. For now it is important to realize that with 30 to 35 million Americans suffering from hypertension, and with hypertension now linked

5

to heart attacks, it is easy to understand why the rate of strokes and heart attacks has increased 300 percent. In addition, the average age of individuals experiencing heart attacks appears to be dropping steadily.[3]

Stress has also been well documented as a main cause of gastrointestinal disorders such as ulcers and colitis. Four million people in the United States suffer from some form of ulcers, and over a million must endure the chronic pain and discomfort of spastic colons.[4] Six million persons have asthma, another stress-linked problem.[5]

Another major physiological result of stress is the headache. The intense pain of a migraine headache can be completely debilitating. Most migraine sufferers can think of no other pain to match it and would try nearly any "cure" to relieve it. Probably 20 million Americans face this pain, some as often as three or four times a week.[6] The cause of migraines is not known for sure, but research has begun to yield a clearer picture of this type of headache. Migraines run in families, and may well be an inherited trait. However, stress appears to be a major precipitator of the actual headache.[7]

What about the more common affliction—the good old-fashioned tension headache? This is the one most of us experience from time to time—as when we are unable to cope in a traffic jam, or when we learn on the same day that our bank account is overdrawn and the public utility company is seeking a 50 percent rate hike. Although normally not as frightening nor as intense as a migraine, the tension headache can be painful, discomforting, and incapacitating.

Stress is a major element in the development of all the medical problems mentioned thus far. This has been long suspected. The only thing that may be new or surprising is the number of people afflicted. Table 1 gives the figures. Even if these were the only diseases that were stress-induced or

Table 1
*Prevalence of Stress-Related Diseases
and Disorders in the United States*

Hypertension	34,290,000
Coronary heart disease	4,240,000
Stroke	1,820,000
Migraine headache	20,000,000
Stomach and duodenal ulcers	4,000,000
Colitis	1,200,000
Asthma	6,000,000
Mental and emotional problems	20,000,000
	91,550,000

stress-aided, the large number of people afflicted would be sufficient justification for the research now being done on stress control. Yet stress and tension are involved in many other disorders—insomnia, hyperactivity, bruxism (grinding one's teeth), and pain. And over 20 million people suffer from such stress-related mental and emotional problems as anxiety and depression.[8] Whether these disorders are purely stress-caused (psychosomatic), stress-aided, or compounded by tension is not always identifiable; but the stress factor cannot be denied or ignored.

THE GERM THEORY

Why are stress and stress-related disorders so prevalent? A satisfactory answer to this question requires that we understand two aspects of the traditional medical approach to treating illness—*crisis intervention* and *the germ theory.*

Crisis intervention means that the physician enters the patient's life *after* the patient has become ill. The patient presents himself to the doctor, who employs a variety of tools and methods to diagnose the illness. Once a diagnosis is made, some form of treatment, usually medication or surgery, is prescribed with the goal of curing the disease. Except for vaccination programs aimed at preventing diseases such as typhoid fever or polio, the medical profession is deeply committed to this crisis-intervention procedure—which might be called illness care.

The germ theory view of disease is a major reason for this practice. Most illnesses are seen as being caused by a germ—some microbe, virus, or infectious agent that contaminates the body to cause illness. If the germ can be identified, then it can be destroyed by powerful drugs and the disease can be cured. Therefore, the way to cure someone who is sick is to destroy the germ causing the illness (or in some cases, to remove or repair destroyed tissue by surgery).

The germ theory has served humanity well. In the early years of this century the leading causes of death in the United States were pneumonia, influenza, and tuberculosis. Other common germ-caused diseases were diphtheria, polio, measles, and mumps. By isolating the virus or germ involved, medical science has developed vaccines and medications that have made polio and diphtheria almost unknown in our society, and today even measles and mumps result only when parents neglect to have their children immunized. These medical advances have spared humanity much illness, suffering, and heartbreak.

In this century, however, there has been a definite shift in disease patterns. Statistics gathered by many sources—from the American Medical Association to the United States Census Bureau—confirm that while infectious, communicable diseases are on the wane, stress-related or degenerative disorders are increasing at an alarming rate. Almost 100 million of us now suffer from some stress-related disorder.

Unfortunately, stress is not caused by a virus or germ. Yet because most medical treatments are based on the germ theory and crisis-intervention model, they enter the picture too late—after the heart attack, the migraine, or the ulcer has appeared. Furthermore, the traditional medical treatments available are often less than effective. Inoculations will not prevent hypertension, heart attacks, ulcers, insomnia, or other stress-related conditions. Surgery cannot remove the stress that caused them, and though medications may ease the symptoms they usually do little to correct the disorders.

In addition to such serious physical disorders, many more people go to their doctors with complaints of anxiety, tension headache, insomnia, or just plain difficult-to-label discomfort. Often, the physician's advice is to "relax." But of course if the patients knew how to relax they wouldn't be patients! Since advice is of little value, the doctor prescribes the one modern-day treatment aimed at stress—the tranquilizer. As a result, *Valium and its derivatives have become the most prescribed drugs in the United States.*[9] This development surely should be seen as a cry from the American public for a more positive and safer way of confronting and solving the problems of stress crisis.

THE HIGH COST OF STRESS

Modern medicine cannot, as yet, cure migraines, heart disorders, anxiety attacks, insomnia, or the whole gamut of stress-related disorders; it can only prescribe medication that will relieve the symptoms. Stop the medication and the symptoms reappear. Take a certain dosage for a period of time and sooner or later that dosage may need to be increased. Take a larger dosage and run the risk of addiction—either physiological or psychological. It becomes a vicious circle; and all the while the cost of medicine continues to rise.

For example, hypertension, a disease linked very closely to stress, is an affliction which can and often does require daily medication. The cost of medication for a typical hypertensive patient is roughly $60 to $70 per month. Such a patient beginning in his early thirties could easily spend during his lifetime a total of $25,000 to $35,000 for medication on this one illness alone. This tremendous burden must be borne by someone—either the patient, his family, or an insurance company (which is one reason for the tremendous increase in premiums for health insurance).

A recent survey showed that the average American family's medicine cabinet contains four prescription drugs.[10] This does not include the host of medications available without a physician's prescription, such as aspirin, sleeping pills, or cough syrup. The survey does not reveal how many of the prescriptions are for stress-related disorders. However, with medical researchers finding that 50 to 85 percent of all illnesses are stress-aided or stress-induced, it can be assumed that many of these drugs are used in an attempt to find relief from stress or stress-caused symptoms—for lowering high blood pressure, for aiding recovery from strokes and heart attacks, for relief of migraines and ulcers, to calm jittery nerves, to help businessmen make it through the day, to help the tired homemaker get a good night's sleep.

Even when psychotherapy is employed, the psychiatrist often finds medication the only available aid to therapy. Hence the tremendous rise in the use of antidepressants, stimulants, and tranquilizers.

THE PHYSIOLOGY OF STRESS

Thus far we have discussed the prevalence of stress, its symptoms, and its cost to society. But what actually is stress? A classical definition can be found in any dictionary. Basically, stress is *pressure or strain on a system.*

Some sources of stress—divorce, loss of a loved one, moving or changing jobs, birth, marriage, raising children, "Christmas syndrome"— create obvious strain and pressure. But there are many more. The widely used Social Readjustment Rating Scale, shown here, rates the relative amount of stress caused by forty-three events which commonly occur in people's lives.[11] Numbers are assigned each event to indicate the amount of stress. The list starts with high-stress events at the top and proceeds to less stressful events at the bottom.

Research suggests that as an individual's total score increases for events that have happened to the person in the last year, so does the likelihood that the person will become ill. The higher the score, the greater the probability that the illness will be serious. Rahe studied 2500 naval officers and enlisted men. The 30 percent with the highest life-change scores developed nearly 90 percent more illnesses during the first month of a cruise than the 30 percent with the lowest scores.[12] And this highest-scoring 30 percent continued to develop more illnesses than the lowest 30 percent during the remainder of the cruise. Another study was of eighty-four physicians.[13] This study used life-change scores for the previous eighteen months as predictors of subsequent illness. Of those with scores over 300, 49 percent reported having illness while only 25 percent of those with 200 to 299 life-change scores and 9 percent with 150 to 199 scores reported any disorders.

Social Readjustment Rating Scale

Event	Value
Death of spouse	100
Divorce	73
Marital separation	65
Jail term	63
Death of close family member	63
Personal injury or illness	53
Marriage	50
Fired from work	47
Marital reconciliation	45
Retirement	45
Change in family member's health	44
Pregnancy	40
Sex difficulties	39
Addition to family	39
Business readjustment	39
Change in financial status	38
Death of close friend	37
Change to different line of work	36
Change in number of marital arguments	35
Mortgage or loan over $10,000	31
Foreclosure of mortgage or loan	30
Change in work responsibilities	29
Son or daughter leaving home	29
Trouble with in-laws	29
Outstanding personal achievement	28
Spouse begins or stops work	26
Starting or finishing school	26
Change in living conditions	25
Revision of personal habits	24
Trouble with boss	23
Change in work hours, conditions	20
Change in residence	20
Change in schools	20
Change in recreational habits	19
Change in church activities	19
Change in social activities	18
Mortgage or loan under $10,000	17
Change in sleeping habits	16
Change in number of family gatherings	15
Change in eating habits	15
Vacation	13
Christmas season	12
Minor violation of the law	11

Not all researchers find a high relationship between major life-change scores and illness.[14] They generally agree that there is a connection between stressful life events and the onset of illness, but point out that the reactions of individuals are so varied that predictions cannot be made for all individuals. A scale like the one shown here can be useful as an indication of tendencies that apply to many, though not all, people.

If in living our lives we had to deal only with these obvious sources of anxiety, and if we also had long periods of time between them to recover, national health statistics might look quite different. Unfortunately, most stress symptoms are linked not to obvious life crises but to small, steady, constantly annoying daily events. To complicate matters further, what causes stress differs from person to person. Happy times can cause as much stress on our systems as difficult times. Rushing a fraternity or sorority, planning for graduation, celebrating a win by your college football team, bidding and making seven no-trump—all can activate the nervous system to the point of overload.*

What occurs physiologically when we experience tension? To see the answer most plainly, consider what happens when we face an extreme form of stress—an unexpected physical threat. Imagine that while cooking at your campsite in the woods, twenty yards from your car, you turn around to see a bear coming at you. You have food in your tent! Or is the bear after you?

Immediately you feel a tightness or churning in your stomach, and a surge of energy flows through you. You must act quickly. Do you fight the bear off with a stick, thus saving your food supply in the tent, or do you run for your car and lock yourself in? Wisely, you run for the car; the bear leaves, and after you have hung your food sack from a distant tree, you can finally relax. Your body has experienced the classical "fight-or-flight" response.

What happened to your system during those first ten or fifteen seconds? How was it instantly made ready to fight or flee? The moment your stress response is triggered (by seeing the bear) your heartbeat quickens to pump more blood to your vital organs. Part of this additional blood is drawn from the peripheral blood vessels lying slightly under the skin throughout the body, leaving you with cold, clammy hands. With the blood drawn away from under your skin, you will not bleed as much if you are cut. As your heartbeat quickens, your blood pressure rises. More blood is received by the muscles and brain—thus enabling you to react more quickly and to think more clearly. Sugar is poured into the system from the liver, supplying quick energy. The adrenal glands pump adrenalin for strength and quickened heart activity. Coagulants are mixed with the blood in order to help stop any

*If you are interested in profiling your reactions to stress in several aspects of your life, consult D. A. Girdano and G. S. Everly, *Controlling Stress & Tension.* (Englewood Cliffs, N.J.: Prentice-Hall, 1979).

bleeding that might occur. The digestive system shuts down so there will be no wasted energy. More red blood cells are produced so the body can utilize additional supplies of oxygen. Stress activates the body's entire mental and physiological systems, precipitating more than 1400 physiological changes. The speed with which this transformation occurs is awesome: in a matter of seconds the body is fully mobilized and ready for action.

When was the last time you used your fight-or-flight response?

When you stepped off the curb before seeing a car coming? When you were threatened by a neighborhood dog while jogging?

In each case, your fight-or-flight response helped you react quickly and save yourself from physical harm—just as it did for your ancestors for thousands of years.

The fight-or-flight response has been developed over millions of years of vertebrate evolution. It was a well-established part of our makeup when our human ancestors still lived in caves and had to deal with saber-toothed tigers. It is still an appropriate response today when we are physically threatened—whether by a bear in the woods or a potential mugger lurking on a deserted street late at night.

Today, however, most of the stress situations we face are not physically life-threatening. Many of the dangers, the daily fight-for-survival situations, have been eliminated. Yet we often react to these modern stress situations as if they were physical threats. Our fight-or-flight response may be triggered even when it is inappropriate. Because there are more stressful situations in modern life, we react more frequently than our ancestors did—with negative consequences as we shall see. Most of these responses may not be full blown fight-or-flight reactions, but significant physiological changes take place nonetheless.

Our *body reacts physiologically* to the mental and emotional concerns in our mind. When we think of an event about which we have some feeling—and we have some feeling or emotion about nearly everything—our physiological system begins to react to that emotion, usually to activate and increase its operation. For most of us, this activation begins first thing in the morning. We wake up pondering the day's activity and our systems respond accordingly. Consider these examples.

A mother who plans on serving her family cereal in the morning is a little late getting started. She goes to the refrigerator and finds there is no milk. What should she prepare now? Her system elevates a little.

A student has a test in one hour. While getting ready to leave for class, he asks himself questions he thinks might be on the test. But the answers do not come readily to mind. He wishes he had studied more. His system elevates as he thinks about taking the test.

While shaving, a man looks out the window and finds three inches of new snow. He had intended to put snow tires on his car last week but never got around to doing it. Now he wonders if he can make it to work on time, knowing he will have to contend with slick streets. His system elevates a little.

A woman, taking her children to school and running her daily errands, constantly recalls her husband's words as he left the house that morning. "Be careful driving today; that back tire looked low last night." That thought nags at her as she tries to complete her errands before taking the car to the garage. Her system begins to elevate.

A man on his lunch hour decides to pick up some dry cleaning downtown. Driving around the crowded block three times he finally spots a vacant parking space. As he approaches, a car dashes around him and slides into what was going to be his space. His foot hits the brake, rage hits his body, and his system elevates.

These examples are only the beginning. The list of situations that affect us physiologically could fill a book. The farmer, homemaker, businessperson, college student, doctor, telephone repairer, contractor, secretary, teacher, all find their days filled with events that cause mental and emotional responses and corresponding physiological responses.

Although common stresses do not overwhelm us, they do elevate our systems frequently, from the first piece of burnt toast in the morning to the minute our exhausted head is lain on the pillow at night. This elevation is what we are working against. Or to be more accurate, it is what is working against us. There would be no long-term problem if we had plenty of time to let our systems return to normal after experiencing an elevation due to stress. Even in the days when our ancestors had to cope with saber-toothed tigers, life-threatening stress situations were not a constant occurrence. There was time to recover from one such situation to the next. Today, however, we often go from one small stress situation to another, throughout the day.

After years of this, our bodily responses begin to take longer and longer to return to normal levels. We lose our ability to recover rapidly. This often results in the elevated state becoming our "normal" state—our blood

---

Which is your most sensitive body system?

Remember the last time you felt "on the spot" or uptight? Where did you feel it in your body? In your stomach? Tense shoulders or jaws? Did your heart pound or your face flush? With practice, you can become aware of very small changes in these body parts. Gaining such awareness is the first step in learning to use biofeedback.

---

pressure is chronically high or more than normal acid is regularly poured into our stomach and causes an ulcer.

Why does one person get high blood pressure, while another gets an ulcer? A number of researchers propose something called *response stereotypy* to explain this.* They say that many people have one physiological system which is more responsive to stress than other systems. This particular system is so sensitive that it is triggered by even a small amount of stress. For example, when a person whose blood pressure is most sensitive and reactive to daily stresses becomes tense, one of the first physiological changes to occur is a rise in blood pressure. It remains elevated until the stimulus passes and then returns to normal. However, when that person's blood pressure is elevated a little, many times a day, day after day and year after year, it tends to normalize at a higher point and establish a new baseline. This results in a gradual but constant rise in blood pressure, and the diagnosis of essential hypertension (high blood pressure with no apparent organic cause) is made.

For others, the muscle system may be the most reactive. They will tend to develop tension headaches, neck or chest pains, low back pains, or general aches and pains throughout the body. For still others it is the gastrointestinal system. When nervous, the stomach rumbles and fills with acid. If agitation of this system continues, the individual may develop ulcers, spastic colon, colitis, or other gastrointestinal disorders. For those who are susceptible in the cardiovascular system, we see the development of high blood

*For more information on this subject, see Johann Stoyva (Department of Psychiatry, University of Colorado Medical Center, Denver, Colorado), "A Psychophysiological Model of Stress Disorders as a Rationale for Biofeedback Training," in E. J. McGuigan, ed., *Tension Control: Proceedings of the Second Annual Meeting of the American Association for the Advancement of Tension Control,* 1976, University Publications, P.O. Box 47, Blacksburg, VA 24060.

pressure, migraines, tachycardia (rapid heart action), and possibly heart attacks and strokes.

PERSONALITY AND STRESS

Our personality also plays some role in how much stress we experience and how that stress affects our bodies. Some types of personalities seem to be more stress prone than others. Two cardiologists from San Francisco, Meyer Friedman and Ray H. Rosenman, got some clues about this from some unexpected sources.[15]

For a long time, they had been studying the relationship of coronary heart disease (CHD) to such factors as smoking, high cholesterol, poor diet, and lack of exercise. But no single factor or combination of factors could be used to predict CHD in their patients with any degree of accuracy.

During this time, they had the chairs in their waiting room reupholstered. The upholsterer commented on the peculiar pattern of wear on the chairs—only the front edges of the seats were worn. The doctors then realized that their patients did not sit back comfortably in the chairs and relax. Rather, they sat on the edges, anxious about their medical condition and undoubtedly impatient at having to wait!

Another clue came during a study of diet, comparing the diets of a group of women with those of their husbands. But diet alone could not explain the fewer heart attacks women had. Then one of the women told the doctors that she knew the reason the husbands had more heart attacks—"The stress they receive in their work, that's what's doing it!"

This sent Rosenman and Friedman off in earnest on a search for the behavior patterns or personality types of persons who are more likely to have heart problems. Over the years, they and subsequent researchers developed descriptions of what has come to be called the Type A behavior pattern.[16]

1. Type A individuals have "hurry sickness" and are very impatient. They can't wait for the stop light to change to green; get agitated if someone holds up the line; are liable to finish sentences for slow talkers; can't waste time even during leisure; set unrealistic deadlines; and so forth.

2. They are very competitive at work and in leisure activities and usually make a contest out of everything, even a friendly game of golf or bowling; they are always competing even when doing their daily jog or swim and cannot play just for fun. They also exhibit aggressive-

ness, usually channeled into ambitious competition, but creeping out at times as hostility and temper.

3. They have an intense drive to accomplish, usually in terms of num- bers—they can (and will) tell you how many dollars they earned, sales made, items produced, cases won; their accomplishments seem more important to them than personal traits.

4. They frequently try to do two or more things at the same time— reading while eating, dictating while driving. This is called *polyphasic behavior.*

In a study covering several years and more than 3000 men, Rosenman and Friedman found that this Type A pattern preceded the development of CHD in about 75 percent of the men in the study.[17]

We are *not* saying that Type A behavior is a response to stress. Rather, it is a personality pattern that results in stress. Unrelenting pressure of time, the constant struggle to achieve more and more in less time and to beat the competition, both in business and leisure activities, results in a kind of stress that seems to overly arouse the cardiovascular system.

People who have this pattern like it! Life would be boring to them if they did not feel constantly challenged—and they wish they had more time to accomplish more. The challenge thus becomes how to help them remain highly energetic without putting so much stress on their bodies.

Another of the more controversial areas of research is that of the possible role of personality in the development of cancer. Is there a pattern of behavior and emotional response that increases the chances of acquiring cancer? Caroline Thomas, a psychologist, began interviewing medical stu- dents at Johns Hopkins in the 1940s. She has interviewed more than 1300 students and kept track of their history of illnesses. Thomas has identified a distinctive psychological profile of the individuals who later developed can- cer. These students reported that they felt a lack of closeness with their parents, that they were "low gear," and only infrequently demonstrated strong emotions.[18]

Lawrence LeShan, another psychologist, studied the histories of more than 500 cancer patients. He also found that their youths were filled with feelings of isolation from their parents and others. Then, in early adult years, they found some meaning in either work or a strong relationship. When this meaning was removed by retirement, death of a spouse, or the like, they experienced feelings of despair, and these feelings were bottled up. LeShan reports that cancer appeared within six months to eight years.[19]

Cancer specialists O. C. Simonton and S. Mathews-Simonton also report a similar pattern—childhood experiences that limited an individual's ability to cope with stresses, then a cluster of stresses over a short period or some critical stress such as retirement or death of a spouse, followed by inability to cope with the stress. The Simontons report that these individuals see themselves as victims of circumstances they are unable to change and as a result they give up, with cancer appearing within six to eighteen months.[20]

The research on personality and heart disease or cancer has encouraged research into personality and other disorders. However, the results are so sketchy at this time that discussion of them must await further work.

Our purpose in presenting this information on personality patterns and their possible relation to specific stress disorders is not to create alarm. Rather, this information suggests that as we become more aware that our lifestyles do affect the level of stress we experience, we can change lifestyles and improve our health. Biofeedback can help us with that enterprise.

SELYE'S GENERAL ADAPTATION SYNDROME

Any discussion of stress should mention the foremost stress researcher, Hans Selye. In 1956 he published *The Stress of Life*, which remains a classic in the field. Stress, as defined by Selye, is a person's response to the demands of his environment.

While a medical student in the 1920s, Selye's interest was aroused by stereotyped responses of the body to demands made upon it. Why did individuals suffering from diverse diseases have so many symptoms in common—diminished appetite, decline in muscular strength, and weight loss? Years later, he began to get some clues from his experiments with rats in the laboratory. To determine how an organism reacts to stress, Selye exposed laboratory animals to a wide variety of extreme stress. He reported that he identified four consistent ways in which these animals responded, regardless of the type of stress: enlargement of the cortex of the adrenal glands; shrinkage of the thymus, spleen, lymph nodes, and other lymphatic structures; nearly total disappearance of eosinophil cells (a kind of white blood cell important to the body's immune response); and bleeding ulcers in the lining of the stomach. This generalized or nonspecific reaction led Selye to define stress as "the nonspecific response of the body to any demand made upon it."

This specific pattern of responses to different stresses Selye called the *general adaptation syndrome* (G.A.S). He states that this syndrome has three stages: (1) the alarm reaction, (2) the stress resistance stage, and (3) the stress exhaustion stage.*

The first stage, the alarm reaction, is the fight-or-flight response.

*For those interested in reading further, Selye gives an annotated bibliography in his book *Stress without Distress* (New York: Lippincott, 1974)

Selye showed that the pituitary hormone ACTH (adrenocorticotrophic hormone) is important in this phase. Increased ACTH secretions stimulate the adrenal cortex to release its hormones, which in turn initiate the G.A.S. When threatened, we are ready to fight or flee. Then, when the danger has passed, our bodies regain their normal physiological balances.

But the stresses of modern times are usually in more subtle forms than threats of physical danger. They are also more frequent. We respond to them with a series of small reactions throughout the entire day. And the sheer number of stress situations means that our bodies do not have time to regain their normal physiological balance. This cumulative stress results in Selye's second stage, stress resistance.

In the stress resistance stage, more distinct changes begin to occur in our bodies. With continued resistance (as stresses continue), parts of our bodies become exhausted. For example, during this stage there often is considerable increase in colds or flu or bacterial infections because the thymus, spleen, and lymphatic organs shrink or begin to atrophy. These organs are important parts of the immune system that protects our bodies against infectious diseases. With prolonged stress, there also are fewer eosinophil cells, those white blood cells that also help protect us against disease-causing microorganisms. It is at this stage that we begin to see patterns emerge, tendencies toward the specific and deadly stress-related disorders described earlier in this chapter.

The amount of energy we have for resistance to stress is limited, and when it is used up the stress exhaustion stage occurs. The body is no longer able to adapt as a total, balanced organism. Imbalances or dysfunctions begin to occur. However, why should we wait for the onset of severe hypertension, coronaries, and other stress-related diseases before we take action? We can learn to avoid the stress exhaustion stage if we can become more aware of physiological cues that precede this state, such as an increasing frequency of headaches, continued heartburn, stomach cramps, or low energy. In fact, with self-regulation training such as that employing biofeedback instruments, we can become more sensitive to the subtle cues that appear even earlier. These cues, which differ from person to person, include slight increases in tension in the neck, lowered skin temperature in the hands, and minor stomach discomfort.

Selye's focus on the generalized physiological responses to stress has sparked numerous debates and more research, resulting in new knowledge about stress. Now, as more is being learned, it becomes apparent that there is more variety than implied originally in the G.A.S—more variety in how our physiology responds to stress, in how stress situations affect our behavior, and in how we perceive potentially stressful events and situations.[21]

OUR PERCEPTIONS TALK

The experience of stress symptoms leads us to a very important point. *Our perception of events causes the physiological changes within our body.* No one can make us angry. No one can hurt our feelings. No one can give us a headache—even though we would like to think so. We do this to ourselves. We perceive the event to be stressful. We read voice intonations into comments and judge them to be hurtful. We control and trigger our own physiological systems—no one else can trigger them for us. We learn our own responses.

We call our finely tuned fight-or-flight response immediately into action when we perceive a physical threat to our life. But we also tend to initiate this same fight-or-flight response when we perceive *nonphysical* threats. We misapply our fight-or-flight reaction to social and interpersonal situations.

When the boss walks in the door, it is we who choose to be nervous. Such a physical response would be appropriate were the boss threatening us physically. He isn't; we perceive his presence as threatening us in nonphysical ways, but we react with tension, activating our fight-or-flight response when there is no actual reason to do so.

When we see a police car behind us, the sudden rush of blood would be appropriate if our life were threatened. It isn't, but we react as if it were. When a train is fifteen minutes late, we mentally become irritated and get our body into the act. When we lose three sets of tennis in a row, we choose to let ourselves forget that it is just a game.

When we choose to interpret a situation as stressful, our body reacts as if the stress were a physical threat and the body systems become stressed, too. Under an overload of continual stress, some of the systems begin to break down. When the breakdown occurs, we become ill. *We have learned to make ourselves sick.*

If we can learn to make ourselves ill, can we reverse the process and learn to make ourselves well? The answer suggested by biofeedback is, "Yes, the process can be reversed." We can learn to regulate our minds and our bodies voluntarily so that we respond appropriately to the stresses in our environment. We can learn to cope effectively with a disorder once it has been contracted and we can even learn to prevent the disorder from occurring.[22]

Let us now examine how biofeedback can teach us to talk to our bodies.

Notes

1 American Heart Association, *Health Facts 1980* (Dallas: National Center, American Heart Association, 1980).

2 Ibid.

3 H. Benson, *The Relaxation Response* (New York: Avon Books, 1975).

4 National Center for Health Statistics, *Prevalence of Selected Digestive Conditions* (Public Health Service, Series 10, No. 123, 1979).

5 National Center for Health Statistics, *National Health Survey* (Public Health Service, Series 10, No. 84, 1973).

6 J. D. Sargent, Head, Migraine Project, The Menninger Foundation, Topeka, KS. Personal communication, 1979. Sargent reports that estimates vary from 15 to 35 million, so 20 million seems a reasonable statistic to report.

7 "Migraine Headache," L. Birk, ed., *Biofeedback: Behavioral Medicine* (New York: Grune and Stratton, 1973).

8 *Report to the President from the President's Commission on Mental Health.* Washington, DC: Superintendent of Documents, 1978. Vol. I, p. 8, reports that the usual estimate is that 10 percent of the population needs mental health services, but that 15 percent would be a more accurate estimate. Thus, 20 million is a conservative estimate. For more specific documentation, see Vol. II, pp. 1–139, "Mental Health: Nature and Scope of the Problems."

9 "The Top 200 Drugs," *Pharmacy Times*, 1980, Vol. 46, pp. 31–39.

10 Oklahoma Drug Workshop, University of Oklahoma, Norman, OK, 1974.

11 T. H. Holmes and R. H. Rahe, "The Social Readjustment Rating Scale," *Journal of Psychosomatic Research*, 1967, Vol. 11, pp. 213–218.

12 R. H. Rahe, "Life-Change Measurement as a Predictor of Illness," *Proceedings of the Royal Society of Medicine*, 1973, Vol. 61, pp. 1124–1126.

13 T. H. Holmes and M. Masuda, "Life Change and Illness Susceptibility," in *Separation and Depression* (Washington, DC: American Association for the Advancement of Science, 1973).

14 H. J. Weshow and G. Reinhart, "Life Change and Hospitalization—A Heretical View," *Journal of Psychosomatic Research*, 1974, Vol. 18, pp. 393–401.

15 M. Friedman and R. H. Rosenman, *Type A Behavior and Your Heart* (New York: Knopf, 1974).

16 For recent summaries, see T. M. Dembroski, "Coronary-Prone Behavior: An Example of a Current Development in Behavioral Medicine," *National Forum*, 1980, Vol. 60, pp. 5–9; also see T. M. Dubroski and others, *Coronary-Prone Behavior* (New York: Wiley, 1981).

17 R. H. Rosenman and others, "Coronary Heart Disease in the Western Collaborative

Group Study: Final Follow-up Experience of 8½ Years," *Journal of the American Medical Association*, 1975, Vol. 8, p. 233.

18 C. B. Thomas and D. R. Duszynski, "Closeness to Parents and the Family Constellation in a Prospective Study of Five Disease States: Suicide, Mental Illness, Malignant Tumor, Hypertension and Coronary Heart Disease," *The Johns Hopkins Medical Journal*, 1974, Vol. 134, pp. 251–270.

19 L. L. LeShan, *You Can Fight for Your Life* (New York: M. Evans, 1977).

20 O. C. Simonton, S. Matthews-Simonton, and J. Creighton, *Getting Well Again* (Los Angeles: J. P. Tarcher, 1978).

21 T. Cox, *Stress* (Baltimore: University Park Press, 1978).

22 E. and A. Green, *Beyond Biofeedback* (New York: Delacorte, 1977); and K. Pelletier, *Mind as Healer, Mind as Slayer* (New York: Delacorte, 1977).

3

ST: SKIN TEMPERATURE
BIOFEEDBACK
TRAINING

Skin temperature (ST) biofeedback is the simplest and most frequently used of all types of biofeedback. Changes in temperature as small as a tenth of a degree or less are detected on the surface of the skin, usually from a fingertip, and fed back by a meter or digital display. We will discuss the instruments and training later in this chapter.

AUTOGENIC TRAINING AND ST FEEDBACK

An accidental finding by three researchers at the Menninger Foundation—Elmer Green, Alyce Green, and Dale Walters—has resulted in the widespread use of ST biofeedback training. Elmer and Alyce Green describe the incident in their book *Beyond Biofeedback*. They were studying how biofeedback might speed up the effects of a therapeutic technique called Autogenic Training, a comprehensive technique for deep relaxation developed in the 1930s by Johannes Schultz, a German psychiatrist.

The initial six stages of Autogenic Training are directed at learning deep physical relaxation. The concept of *passive concentration* helps in the training—letting the sensations of deep relaxation come over a person rather than actively striving for them. The first stage is learning to feel heaviness in the limbs, a sensation associated with muscle relaxation. It begins by the trainee silently repeating the phrase, "My right arm is heavy" while attending passively to the arm. The person stays with this "heavy" formula until able to feel heaviness throughout the limbs, which may happen almost immediately or take one or two weeks of training. The second stage of training uses formulas focusing on warmth, a subjective sensation also associated with relaxation. Four to eight weeks are usually required to achieve sensations of warmth in the extremities. The remaining four stages focus on phrases to establish regular heartbeat ("My heartbeat is calm and regular"), respiration pattern ("It breathes me"), warmth in the abdominal area ("My solar plexis is warm"), and relaxation of the forehead ("My forehead is cool"). Two months to a year of training are usually required to be able to achieve the desired responses to the entire series of six stages in three or four minutes.

The second series of six stages trains in *autogenic meditation*. A series of visualization exercises helps develop abilities to resolve stress-related disorders such as asthma, headaches, insomnia, frequent constipation, stuttering, bed-wetting, and psychological problems such as anxieties and phobias. A comprehensive report of the system and the extensive research it has stimulated is found in a three-volume work by Wolfgang Luthe, a student of Schultz's and the recognized authority on Autogenic Training.[1]

The Greens were testing the phrases designed for physical relaxation. As part of their research, thirty-three women were wired to instruments to measure a number of physiological processes, including heart rate, respiration, skin temperature, blood flow in the hands, and galvanic skin response. They were then given Autogenic Training phrases for relaxing the body and warming the hands, to be followed by two weeks of practice at home. Elmer Green describes the events:

> Our most interesting findings led to the use of voluntary hand warming for control of migraine headache. It came about accidentally. One of the subjects developed a migraine headache during both her laboratory sessions, brought on, she said, by fear that she would not succeed in warming her hands. During the second lab session, after the Autogenic Training practice and the ensuing fear and headache, we asked the subject to run through another simple test routine, which was part of the research design: to watch a small light for ten minutes in a totally darkened, quiet room. It was very relaxing. All she had to do was touch a switch if the light appeared to move. While this was going on, I was in the instrument room, studying the physiological records as they emerged on the polygraph. Suddenly, at about the ninth minute, I noticed a rapid vasodilation in both hands, and a corresponding increase in hand temperature of about

10°F in the next two minutes. When the test was over I went into the experimental room and asked, "What happened to you a couple of minutes ago?" She replied, "How did you know my headache went away?"[2]

Shortly after this event, the wife of a research colleague asked if she could be "trained out of migraine." The principle of combining Autogenic Training phrases with biofeedback training was explained and she was conducted through a fifteen-minute training session. She was given a copy of the phrases, a portable temperature feedback instrument, and told to train every day and to call at the end of a week.

After two weeks of training, she had stopped taking her medications and did not need the instrument; she did not have a migraine for the next ten years. Her ability to turn down her fight-or-flight system allowed her to live fully but in a more relaxed style without inducing migraines. This accidental finding, suggesting the possibility of biofeedback training as a treatment for migraines, resulted in much subsequent research and the establishment of the efficacy of the treatment, as we shall discuss later.

In migraine-prone persons, there appears to be a constriction of blood vessels in the scalp followed by an excessive dilation. Learned reactions to the normal stresses of everyday life trigger the response that results in a headache. This process is accompanied by a *decrease* of blood flow to the hands, resulting in colder hands. Skin temperature training to increase the warmth of the hands, by increasing the flow of blood to the hands, affects subcortical neural centers which rebalance the entire vascular system of the body.[3] Thus biofeedback training to warm hands has become a therapeutic technique for many migraine sufferers.

Migraine Headaches

Skin temperature biofeedback training can relieve migraine headaches, but the goal of training is to learn how to *avoid* bringing on migraine headaches. A migraine-prone person might spend five minutes warming his or her hands before getting out of bed in the morning—without biofeedback instruments—just by using the mental-emotional-physical strategies that the person has learned while practicing with the instruments. In addition, repeating the practice several times during the day seems sufficient for many. During those brief sessions, attention is focused inward to spot internal signs of tension. The tension is released, perhaps by two slow inhalations and exhalations. The person learns to go through the day managing the usual daily events and activities without building up unnecessary tension levels which in turn may trigger the migraine. For most of the 20 million migraine sufferers in the United States, biofeedback, *when properly understood and used,* can result in substantial relief or elimination of the headaches.

The success rate usually quoted for ST biofeedback training for migraines comes from the studies of an internist at the Menninger Foundation, Joseph Sargent. Interested in the accidental discovery of the Greens and Dale Walters, he has since directed a long-standing treatment and research project. He uses the combination of autogenic phrases and biofeedback training developed by the Greens. Results of Sargent's initial research with seventy-five persons with migraines suggested that 60 to 75 percent benefited from ST biofeedback training, augmented with autogenic phrases.[4] There have been numerous studies of ST training with migraine sufferers since the serendipitous finding by the Greens. These studies have been summarized in a special task force report by the Biofeedback Society of America entitled *Biofeedback in the Treatment of Vascular Headache.*[5] Some of the research reports success rates equal to those of Sargent, while other research reports lower rates. Thus, there is no definitive answer as yet to just how successful biofeedback training is with those suffering from migraines. More research is needed to better understand the effects of such factors as attitudes of the trainer, expectations of both the trainer and the migraine sufferer, differences in readiness to learn biological self-regulation, and possible differential effects with different kinds of migraine headaches.

The Greens have noted an interesting pattern, corroborated by persons working in biofeedback clinics across the country. Some individuals training with ST learn to control their migraines and then lose that ability. In the course of their biofeedback training, these individuals frequently become aware of some difficult situation in their lives that the migraines help to manage. That is, the migraines represent a successful, if painful, way of coping. When the problem is recognized and faced, some decide that the migraines are too important to give up, so they do not regain their control over them. Others decide to change the way they cope with the problem. When that decision is made, the ability to control the headache usually returns.

Raynaud's Disease

Raynaud's disease is a disorder of the blood vessels, usually in the hands and feet. An attack is brought on by cold stimulation (picking up a cold pop bottle, being out in cold weather) or emotional stress. In severe cases, the fingers or toes turn white and then blue as spasms in the blood vessels restrict circulation. As the constriction recedes, there is an excess flow of blood before the vessels return to normal, often a painful process to experience.

ST feedback has been used with a number of persons suffering from Raynaud's disease, and generally with success. One of the first reports was of a fifty-year-old woman who had a thirty-year history of the disorder. She first was taught relaxation and Autogenic Training, and then trained on skin temperature biofeedback. She practiced ST feedback training ten minutes twice a day for a month. She then reported that she could grasp the cold steering wheel of her car without gloves for the first time in thirty years.[6]

Another interesting report is of a woman who had a long history of migraines. These disappeared after an automobile accident, but Raynaud's disease appeared. It was severe enough that she had sores on the tips of her fingers. She had five days of practice with an ST biofeedback training instrument, and then returned home and practiced without the instrument several times a day. Three weeks later she reported being able to shovel snow and said she was able to type again for the first time in many years. Several months later she reported being out in below zero weather without her hands turning blue.[7]

Case reports such as these are tantalizing, but they do not prove the efficacy of ST biofeedback training for Raynaud's disease since most of the published reports have been of individual cases. However, a task force report of the Biofeedback Society of America which summarizes research involving 130 persons with Raynaud's disease[8] concludes that ST biofeedback training has been shown to be very promising as a treatment for the disorder. The report notes that existing conventional treatments are generally unsatisfactory because they have minimal effects on the disorder or unpleasant side effects (medication), or are quite radical (surgery). In contrast, no undesirable side effects have been observed with ST training.

Hypertension

Hypertension is a very serious problem. In most instances, the disorder is not related to any other physical problem, and is called essential hypertension. The medication for hypertension is expensive, and many individuals suffer from strong side effects, such as itching or some loss in mental alertness.

Most of the reported research on biofeedback treatment for hypertension has used a special cuff on the arm that gives frequent blood pressure feedback.[9] ST feedback training is also being used as a treatment.

The Biofeedback and Psychophysiological Clinic of the Menninger Foundation has been conducting pioneering work using ST biofeedback training with hypertensive persons (persons having blood pressure over 140/90; normal is 120/80). Emphasis is placed on ST training, first from a finger, by attaching a temperature sensor called a thermistor, which is connected to a biofeedback machine. Home practice is a minimum of three times daily, using the ST biofeedback instrument, with logs to be filled out that emphasize self-awareness of feelings and sensations associated with warmer hands. As an individual relaxes, the hands tend to get warmer. Thus, through this method, the trainees learn how to maintain deeper relaxation throughout the day, while still carrying on their daily activities. When a trainee can maintain finger temperatures over 95.5°F for ten minutes or more in the office of the trainer, training is shifted to the feet. The thermistor is attached to the bottom of the big toe, and home training concentrating on this area continues for a minimum of three times daily. Autogenic-type phrases are taught, as is a simple breathing technique called *equalized breathing*, or making inhalations and exhalations of equal duration (many individuals tend to have shorter exhalations). Approximately five of the office training sessions also use EMG (muscle tension) feedback training to enhance general relaxation.

Fifty-two persons have completed this program. Thirty-one were on medication. Of these, 87.5 percent have demonstrated complete success at achieving normotensive levels (blood pressure less than 140/90) while reducing medication levels to zero. Of the twenty-one hypertensives who were not on medication, 93.8 percent reached normotensive levels.[10] Other biofeedback clinics are beginning to use this program and their results, when published, should give a better indication of how successful this process actually is by providing a larger data base.

At the Biofeedback Clinic, this procedure required an average of twenty weeks of training for blood pressure to return to normal without the aid of medication, with a range from five to sixty-eight weeks. Considering that an individual spends years developing behaviors that contribute to high blood pressure, to learn in a matter of months how to live and keep one's blood pressure down is quite a feat.

Another practitioner uses ST feedback combined with some nutritional changes and reports that he frequently observes drops of over 15 percent.[11] For example, an Air Force pilot had blood pressure averaging 130/110. A few weeks of ST feedback resulted in an average of 122/80. His blood pressure was taken frequently and averaged 118/84 after termination of the biofeedback training.

More dramatic is a report of a woman with blood pressure of 185/125. In addition to nutritional changes, she trained to increase her skin temperature, particularly in the upper arm region where blood pressure typically is measured. After several weeks she was able to increase her skin temperature from approximately 78°F to 93°F and her blood pressure had dropped to 125/80 with medication, a drop that she had been unable to attain with medication alone. When her medication was reduced, her pressure went back up to about 165/110. With additional training, her pressure came down to between 140/90 and 125/80 and she had decreased her medication by two-thirds. There are no reports of this combination of ST training and nutrition being used at other clinics, so there are no additional data on this intriguing technique and present results must be labeled tentative.

Other Applications of ST

ST biofeedback training has shown promise in a number of other areas. More research will be needed, but the initial results are promising enough to warrant a further look. One such area is the effects of ST feedback training on speaking behavior.[12] One group of students used skin temperature training instruments and practiced increasing hand temperature while imagining themselves giving their final impromptu speech before the entire group. A second group of students did everything the first group did, except for practicing with the feedback instruments. Speeches recorded before and after training were analyzed. The ST biofeedback trained group did significantly better than the other group on specific measures of speaking behavior.

ST training also has been used with women with a history of menstrual cramps. Research suggests that about 80 percent may achieve considerable relief as a result of the training.[13] Relaxation in the hands results in vasodilation of the blood vessels and warmer skin temperatures. Apparently these women were using the skills learned in achieving relaxation in the hands to help relax and ease tensions associated with menstrual cramps.

A case study has been reported in which ST training was used to help an individual overcome insomnia.[14] Using the mental strategies associated with warmer hands helped this person overcome insomnia-inducing thoughts and substitute sleep-inducing mental states. Again, we should note that this is only one case study and therefore is not conclusive.

ST training has been used as part of a rehabilitation program for sixty-eight prisoners.[15] Eight sessions of ST training were followed by seventeen hours of group sessions which included heavy use of visualizations and guided imagery designed to explore self-concepts. The experimenter felt that the prisoners' success in ST training was accompanied by an increased sense of self-mastery, which permitted a more honest and open exploration of ideas designed to bring about changes in self-image. Of these sixty-eight prisoners in the study, sixty-two were released. Eight of the sixty-two, or 12.9 percent, were later returned to prison. This figure compares with a recidivism rate of 35.6 percent for the state in which this research was conducted. Again, this research is suggestive, but it does not delineate how much of the change was due to the biofeedback training, how much to the other aspects of the treatment, or how much just to the attention the prisoners were receiving. It does suggest, though, that more work is justified in the use of ST biofeedback training in this area

Some other versatile uses have been reported that combined nutrition and skin temperature biofeedback training for treating such diverse problems as rheumatoid arthritis and bursitis, diabetes, hypoglycemia, hypothyroidism, chronic pain, and anxiety.[16] These uses are in very preliminary stages of development, and only a few biofeedback trainers are using them.

All of these applications used skin temperature biofeedback instruments giving immediate and continuous feedback. Using such instruments, individuals are able to do different internal experiments and get immediate feedback of the results. They learn what internal thoughts and emotions are associated with increases or decreases in skin temperature (with increased relaxation and blood flow to the fingers, or increased tension and blood flow away from the fingers). What follows is a description of the biofeedback instruments and some training strategies.

INSTRUMENTS FOR
ST BIOFEEDBACK TRAINING

Skin temperature biofeedback instruments use a detector or sensor called a thermistor for measuring temperature changes. The thermistor is usually taped over the fingerprint of the middle finger of the right hand for right-

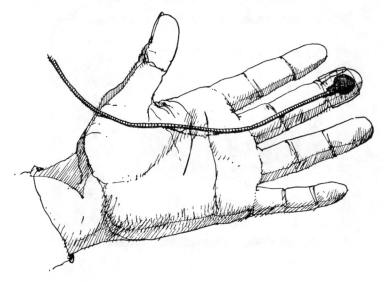

Figure 1 *Skin temperature biofeedback instruments use u sensor or thermistor for measuring temperature changes. The most frequent placement is over the fingerprint of the middle finger of the dominant hand.*

handed individuals and the left hand for left-handed individuals. Figure 1 shows the placement of the thermistor. It is taped on comfortably so that it does not restrict the flow of blood. When practicing, care must be taken not to press the thermistor against anything and to avoid squeezing it between the thumb and finger. To do so tends to mask out the small changes in temperature that are crucial to successful ST biofeedback training.

The thermistor transmits the surface temperature of the skin through a wire to the biofeedback machine, which then translates the signal from the thermistor into a feedback signal for the trainee. This signal reflects the skin temperature and any variations that occur.

Most instruments use a meter for feeding back skin temperature. The meter is calibrated so that each line on the scale represents a change of only one-tenth of a degree Fahrenheit, as shown in Figure 2. Controls on the instrument enable a person training to determine the exact surface temperature of the finger and to watch as the temperature increases or decreases.

Other instruments use digital feedback displays ranging in size from those found in pocket calculators to those found in digital clocks. Most show temperature changes of as little as one-tenth of a degree, with a few showing changes as small as one-hundredth of a degree, as in Figure 3.

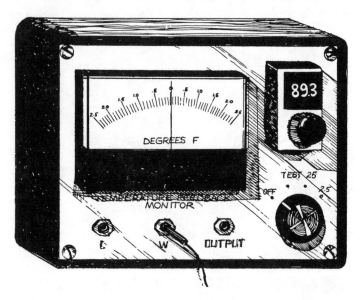

Figure 2 *Most skin temperature biofeedback instruments use a meter. These meters are calibrated so that each line represents a change of one-tenth (0.1) of a degree.*

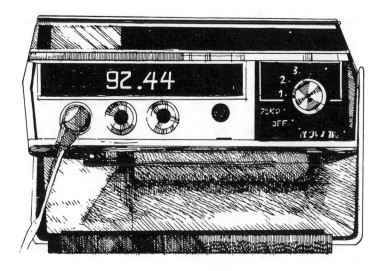

Figure 3 *Some skin temperature biofeedback instruments use digital feedback displays. Most digital displays show changes in tenths of a degree, with a few showing changes as small as one-hundredth of a degree.*

It is important that temperature biofeedback instruments give feedback of changes in temperature of less than a degree, preferably of a tenth of a degree or less. Such sensitive feedback is extremely helpful to those training with the instruments. Also, the instruments must be capable of reacting quickly so that changes can be seen on the meter or digital readout as soon after they occur as possible. Naturally, this feedback must be accurate. At the time of this writing, temperature feedback instruments that meet these requirements range in price from $125 for home training instruments to $250 or more for clinical and laboratory models.

All biofeedback machines described in this book are safe. One feels no electrical shock or other pain while hooked to a biofeedback instrument. Most of the instruments are battery operated, thus eliminating any chance of shock. Because of the design, there is no discomfort whatsoever in their use.

An inexpensive, cardboard-backed thermometer, about three inches long, can be used in conjunction with the training being done with a biofeedback clinician. This thermometer can be used at home to practice what is being learned in the training with the professional. The cardboard back should be cut off just above the bulb and the thermometer taped to the finger,

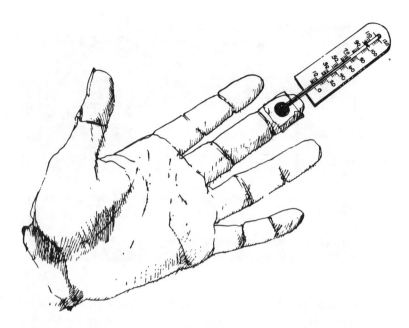

Figure 4 *An inexpensive, cardboard-backed thermometer can be used for home practice. The cardboard back is cut off just above the bulb and the thermometer taped to the finger.*

as in Figure 4. Though not as precise as ST biofeedback instruments, a cardboard-backed thermometer can give feedback that can help an individual achieve voluntary self-regulation.

The taped thermometer can be used to check on one's surface temperature in different situations throughout the day. Higher temperatures indicate more relaxed states and cooler temperatures indicate more tense states. Changes in the readings on the thermometer give a person feedback showing how he or she is reacting in various situations. This results in feedback about how well the person is applying, throughout the day, the temperature feedback training.

INITIAL HOOK-UP AND TRAINING

The first session of biofeedback training is often looked upon with some skepticism, a little reluctance, and usually a great deal of hope. Because it is so different from other types of treatment, individuals usually get a better understanding of how biofeedback works and the active role they will need to take in the training when the procedure is explained before the actual "hooking up."

The goal of ST biofeedback training is for the trainee to learn to increase and decrease finger skin temperature voluntarily, and to do this eventually without monitoring with the biofeedback instrument. A goal for most trainees is to be able to increase finger skin temperature to more than 95.5°F and hold it at that level for several minutes while carrying on a conversation. This temperature level generally denotes deep physical relaxation, usually accompanied by a more passive mental state.

To begin training, a person sits in a chair, hands resting on the lap, facing the temperature biofeedback instrument, as shown in Figure 5. After noting the baseline or initial temperature, the person begins training to raise hand temperature. A number of techniques are available to aid the individual's progress.

One technique is to leave the person alone to discover the thoughts or feelings which seem to relate to and regulate that person's own particular finger temperature and blood flow. Although some success is reported using

Figure 5 *When training, a person usually sits in a chair, hands resting in the lap, facing the skin temperature biofeedback instrument.*

this trial-and-error discovery method, most biofeedback trainers provide the trainee more specific help.

Self-Directing Phrases
and Visualizations

Trainers working with Elmer and Alyce Green at the Menninger Foundation use self-directing phrases based on those employed in Autogenic Training. Early in the training, the phrases are read to the trainee with time between phrases for silently imagining them taking place. Later, the trainee repeats the phrases to himself while visualizing or imagining them happening.

Examples of such phrases are: "I am very quiet . . . My feet are heavy and warm . . . My hands, my arms, and my shoulders feel heavy, relaxed, and comfortable . . . My hands are warm . . . Warmth is flowing into my hands; they are warm, warm . . . My thoughts are turned inward and I am at ease."

Another commonly used technique is visualization. Visualization is the process of closing one's eyes and imagining a picture of things, events, or feelings. These can be visualizations that bring feelings of relaxation or contentment or ones that bring tension, frustration, and anxiety.

When first training with skin temperature feedback, a person will be trying to learn to warm his hands. He may visualize the hand being lowered into a bucket of warm water, or the image might be of holding the hands out over a warm fire. The image might even be more general, such as imagining lying on a warm beach being drenched by a hot sun, or taking a sauna.

One of the most creative visualizations we have run across was that of the student who imagined that the thermistor on her finger was a bunch of carrots and that her blood cells were rabbits running down her arm to eat the carrots. When she imagined this, her finger temperature went up rapidly, and she became more relaxed.

The effect of visualization on the physiological functions of the body has long been recognized. The body tends to respond to what the mind is concentrating on, for it is from the mind that the body takes most of its cues.

To confirm this fact, the next time you are watching an exciting movie and there is a thrilling chase scene or very emotional moment occurring on the screen, withdraw yourself from it and check your body tension level. Most likely you will find yourself leaning forward a little, fists or teeth slightly clenched, arm and leg muscles tense, and breathing faster than usual. Your body is reacting to what you are witnessing. You are physiologically preparing to meet the same challenge that is being met on the screen. Your body is not discriminating that you are only an observer of the scene and not a participant. This is why it is perfectly possible that watching television all evening, far from being relaxing, can leave you too wound up to sleep!

If further proof of the effect of visualization is needed, do this short exercise. Close your eyes for a moment and try to think of absolutely nothing. Just let your mind go blank and rest quietly for fifteen or twenty seconds. Now imagine a lemon. A nice, ripe lemon. And now imagine biting into this wonderfully tart fruit. Keep biting and sucking this lemon in your mind for several seconds. Now check your body. Are your lips puckered? Are your jaws clenched? What about the muscles in your arms and shoulders? How about your eyes? Are you squinting? Physiologically you are reacting to what your mind is picturing. The nearest lemon may still be in the supermarket, but not according to your body.

If you can teach yourself to be tense by visualization, you can teach yourself to relax by visualization. The biofeedback equipment aids you in your progress.

Discovering Internal States

Regardless of the technique used in conjunction with the temperature training instrument, certain points should be remembered. First, the trainee is attempting to discover the particular internal feelings or emotional states that are associated with different temperatures. At the beginning of training, several strategies are tried to see what effects each has on the feedback. By experimenting in this way the trainee comes to better understand what a particular action does to his system. He can then practice rejecting the undesired response and repeating the desired response, thereby learning the skills needed to control this particular physiological function.

The second point to remember is that in learning this process a very casual attitude should be maintained during practice sessions. In attempting to raise skin temperature, it is better to think "I'll let it happen" than "I'll make it happen."

One of the commonest mistakes made during early practice sessions is trying too hard. Paradoxical as it seems, if we imagine or think about the body doing something and then let it happen, it will; but if we tell the body to do something and then try to force it to occur, very often it won't. How many times have you told yourself, "I'm not going to be nervous in this situation," only to find that the harder you try not to be, the more nervous you become? By simply letting it happen, or using "passive volition," as Alyce and Elmer Green refer to it, the desired result can be obtained much sooner.

How long it might take you to re-regulate the vascular system, and the degree to which this control is mastered, will depend on several variables, including your faithfulness to the exercises, the condition of your vascular system, and your ability to incorporate into your daily life what is being learned in training.

Nevertheless, some degree of voluntary self-regulation is nearly always possible. In most instances, for example, an individual is able to learn some control in raising at least hand temperature. While this in itself is only a first step toward self-regulation it is an indication of future progress that may be made.

As a person learns to raise hand temperature, certain general body feelings are noted during the practice time. Often there is a heaviness in the arms and legs, and later throughout the entire body. A definite feeling of warmth may be noted, and many people even experience a sensation in which they feel their limbs are floating in space.

For most people, an increase in hand temperature seems to be accompanied by relaxation throughout the entire body. This feeling may be associated with mental images or sometimes musical notes flowing through the mind. Some individuals panic a little when they begin to experience this complete relaxation during their training because they feel they are losing control. Actually, they are not. They are beginning to learn true control—the ability to tense or to relax at will. After experiencing such deep relaxation many people learn to let go and to reach this point again and again at will, without feedback instruments.

Notes

1 W. Luthe, ed., *Autogenic Training*, Vols. 1–3 (New York: Grune & Stratton, 1969).

2 E. and A. Green, *Beyond Biofeedback* (New York: Delacorte, 1977), p. 35.

3 *Ibid.*, p. 37.

4 J. D. Sargent, E. E. Green, E. D. Walters, "Preliminary Report on the Use of Autogenic Feedback Training in the Treatment of Migraine and Tension Headaches," *Psychosomatic Medicine*, 1973, Vol. 35, pp. 129–135.

5 S. Diamond, J. Diamond-Falk, and T. DeVeno, "Biofeedback in the Treatment of Vascular Headache" (Task Force Report of the Biofeedback Society of America), *Biofeedback and Self-Regulation*, 1978, Vol. 3, pp. 385–408.

6 E. Peper, Case report described in R. S. Surwit, "Biofeedback: a Possible Treatment for Raynaud's Disease," chapter in L. Birk, ed., *Biofeedback: Behavioral Medicine* (New York: Grune and Stratton, 1973).

7 E. and A. Green, *Beyond Biofeedback*, p. 41.

8 E. Taub and C. F. Stroebel, "Biofeedback in the Treatment of Vasoconstrictive Syndromes" (Task Force Report of the Biofeedback Society of America), *Biofeedback and Self-Regulation*, 1978, Vol. 3, pp. 363–373.

9 D. A. Williamson and E. P. Blanchard, "Heart Rate and Blood Pressure Biofeedback, I. A Review of the Recent Experimental Literature. *Biofeedback and Self-Regulation*, 1979, Vol. 6, pp. 1-36.

10 S. Fahrion and others, *Biobehavioral Approaches to the Treatment of Hypertension: A Research Proposal*. Submitted to the Behavioral Medicine Branch of the Heart, Lung and Blood Institute, Washington, D.C., June, 1980.

11 G. Eversaul, *Practical and Potential Applications of Feedback Thermometer Training and Nutrition in Crisis and Preventive Medicine*. Mimeographed, 3201 Maryland Parkway No. 428, Las Vegas, NV, 1974.

12 C. E. Tapie Rohm, R. Sorenson, and J. D. Gibbs. "Biofeedback Hand Temperature Training and Speaking Behavior," *Proceedings of the Biofeedback Research Society, 1976* (Denver: Biofeedback Research Society, 1976).

13 W. Tubbs and C. Carnahan, "Clinical Biofeedback for Primary Dysmenorrhea: A Pilot Study," *Proceedings of the Biofeedback Research Society, 1976;* and K. Sedlacek and M. Heczey, "A Specific Biofeedback Treatment for Dysmenorrhea," *Proceedings of the Biofeedback Society of America, 1977.* In 1976 the Biofeedback Research Society changed its name to Biofeedback Society of America.

14 J. K. Benjamins and W. D. Schofield, "Treatment of Sleep Onset Insomnia with Finger Temperature Feedback and Self-Monitoring: A Case Study," *Proceedings of the Biofeedback Society of America, 1978.*

15 P. Norris, *"Working with Prisoners, or There's Nobody Else Here,"* unpublished doctoral dissertation, 1976.

16 G. Eversaul, *Practical and Potential Applications.*

EMG: MUSCLE TENSION BIOFEEDBACK TRAINING

Do you suffer from tension headaches? Insomnia? Are you afraid of riding in elevators? Afraid of heights? Are you a teeth-grinder? Or have you lost the use of some muscles from an accident or a stroke? These are just some of the areas in which electromyographic (EMG) biofeedback training is being used.

An electromyographic biofeedback instrument gives feedback about what is happening in a particular group of muscles, such as those in the forearm or forehead. This feedback is usually both visual (by a meter) and auditory (by clicking sounds that speed up with more tension and slow down with relaxation). With this feedback and with practice, a person can learn to voluntarily relax particular muscle groups or tense muscles that contribute to the stress-related difficulties just mentioned.

HOW EMG TRAINING WORKS

When muscles function properly, a series of electrical impulses is transmitted to the muscle fibers. As these electrical impulses pass over the nerve endings, a contraction or tightening of the muscle occurs. When there is a decrease in electrical activity, muscle relaxation occurs. Thus, the more electrical activity occurring within a muscle bundle the more tense the muscle; less electrical activity means more relaxed muscles. These electrical impulses are very weak and are measured in microvolts, or millionths of a volt. As a comparison, an

Figure 6 *For EMG biofeedback training, electrical activity related to muscle-tension changes is detected by electrodes. A frequent placement is on the forehead. Auditory feedback is by headphones.*

electrical light bulb uses 120 volts. EMG biofeedback training for deep relaxation usually involves picking up these tiny signals in the 1 to 20 microvolt range, although in rehabilitation medicine, the range might be in the hundreds of microvolts. In any case, precise instruments are needed to detect these tiny impulses and filter out other unrelated electrical activity.

The electrical activity of the muscle is detected by the use of electrodes placed on the skin directly over the muscle being monitored, as shown in Figure 6.

The EMG signal is usually fed back by auditory and visual means. Audio feedback involves clicks that speed up as muscle tension increases and slow down as the muscle relaxes. Visual feedback (Figure 7) is usually either by means of a meter giving continuous readings in microvolts or a series of lights indicating tensing or relaxing.

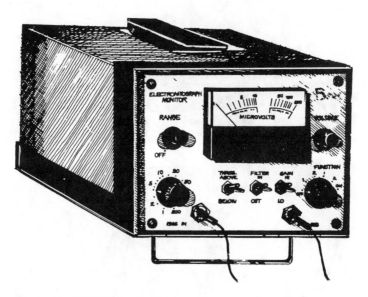

Figure 7 *EMG biofeedback instruments give visual feedback of muscle activity, usually by a meter giving continuous readings of microvolt levels.*

INITIAL HOOK-UP AND TRAINING

EMG biofeedback training begins by attaching the electrodes over a muscle. Let us say it is the extensor muscle (the one on the top of the forearm). Tension and relaxation of this muscle can easily be demonstrated by clenching and relaxing the fist. This allows the person to understand the workings of the EMG machine before moving on to the more difficult-to-control muscle groups.

Many biofeedback trainers begin EMG training by going directly to the forehead muscles (called the frontal area) for the initial hook-up. If the level of tension in this area is high and the individual has difficulty getting some success in lowering the tension level, then the electrodes will be moved back to the forearm extensor muscle for training. The experience of biofeedback trainers is that it is easier to learn voluntary self-control of this muscle and the strategies learned in training with it help in training with the forehead muscles.

Without taking EMG training, many people—perhaps including you —believe that they can already voluntarily lower the level of tension in their forearm or forehead to nearly completely relaxed levels. Such is not usually the case. We could hook you up to an EMG instrument, have you lie on the floor, and have you give us a signal when you think your tensions were nearly all gone from these muscles. Were we to turn the EMG meter so you could see it, you might be surprised at how much tension still remained.

The level of tension in these forehead muscles varies greatly from person to person. Also, the rate at which people learn to increase their voluntary control of these muscles varies widely, from those requiring just a few sessions to others requiring many weeks.

For many persons, learning to lower the level of tension in the forehead may be accompanied by lower tension levels in other parts of the body, along with mental and emotional unstressing. Control of the forehead muscles for others might be followed by training with the electrodes placed on the neck muscles and later the shoulder muscles. Most of the time, control of these three sets of muscles will bring about a general state of mental, emotional, and physical relaxation.

Once control of these muscles has been achieved, the electrodes are placed directly over any muscles still at high tension levels. For instance, in cases of low back pain the electrodes can be placed over the various muscles within the affected area. This allows the trainee to gain more complete control over a particular set of tense muscles.

RELAXATION TRAINING TECHNIQUES FOR EMG

Several techniques are employed to help the trainee gain control of his muscles. The same type of Autogenic Training and visualization employed in ST training may be used in EMG training. By relaxing and bringing warmth to the skin, tense muscles oftentimes will correspondingly relax. However, as with nearly all statements about biofeedback training, there are exceptions. Some people demonstrate excellent control with the ST training instrument and can produce high hand temperature, but they nevertheless retain high tension levels within their muscles. This is probably because two different body systems are involved: the autonomic nervous system for blood flow, and the craniospinal nervous system for muscle tension. Training for voluntary control in one system does not necessarily mean that control carries over to the other.

Other techniques are used in conjunction with the autogenics and visualization, such as training in tensing and relaxing. The trainee tenses a group of muscles (such as the fist) and studies how that tension feels. Then the muscles are relaxed—"let go"—and slowly drift toward a more normal state. This allows the person both to gain greater awareness of his muscles as he goes about daily activities and to be more aware of what tension feels like, so he can become conscious of letting his tensions go during the day. The process of tensing and relaxing a muscle is repeated for all muscle groupings in the body, including the scalp, face, neck and shoulders, back, chest, abdomen, arms, legs, and feet.

Trainees are encouraged to work out their own strategies. As with all biofeedback training, what works varies tremendously. One person imagined skiing in Colorado and the EMG readings from his forehead went down to about as low as possible. For some, this visualization would be tensing, but this person found skiing to be a real release. Someone else imagined turning inside her head and "shutting off the power" at a control center in the middle of her brain. Or one might imagine a blank blackboard, so that when a thought appears on it, it can be mentally erased. Another strategy might be to become aware just of the rising and falling of one's chest while breathing, or the air flowing in and out at the tip of the nose. Some individuals focus on a thought. Each person, though, will try different strategies, and the feedback will help identify what works.

Individuals who have suffered from a stroke can learn to *increase* the levels of tension in their muscles. They use strategies different from those based on relaxation and letting go. They might imagine working on a difficult problem, kicking a ball, recalling past events that involved the muscle groups being trained, or using special exercises to try to get movement in a particular group of muscles.

No matter what the intended purpose, EMG training requires much practice. Training with the instrument is from one to several times a week, plus home practice regularly without the instrument. As voluntary control improves, practice throughout the day, for brief periods, is added. Many people establish set times for their brief practice periods—when stopped at a traffic light, waiting for an elevator, letting the phone ring two more times while taking a deep breath and letting it out slowly, when television programs change, or at any convenient time. Through regular practice, a person is able to keep his muscle tension level from building and is able to deal with the normal stresses of daily life without overreacting. As more than one successful EMG trainee has concluded, "Now I'm in control!"

SPECIFIC APPLICATIONS OF EMG

Some persons are able to learn exquisitely fine control of muscles by EMG biofeedback training. Just how finely was demonstrated by one of the leaders in muscle tension feedback training research, John Basmajian.[1]

Check yourself the next time you are driving and have to stop for a red light. Do you fidget and fuss? You'll probably be sitting there for thirty seconds with no place to go. Instead of making yourself more tense by becoming aggravated, use the time to drop your tension level. Turn your head as far to the right and left as you can, not too fast. Do the same with your eyes. Now take a slow deep breath, let it out, check the traffic, and proceed with the green light more relaxed, but alert.

Some of the subjects in his research learned to activate muscles voluntarily to produce rhythms that sounded like a variety of horse gallops, or rhythms that sounded like drums beating. This was accomplished by controlling a tiny part of a muscle called a *single motor unit* (SMU), the few muscle fibers controlled by a *single nerve cell*. Muscles are made up of bundles of tiny muscle fibers that are triggered by weak electrical impulses. A muscle, then, is many muscle fibers commanded by many nerve cells.

Basmajian used tiny electrodes attached to the muscle at the base of the thumb. The subjects in his research had to learn to control the firing of all the nerve cells to the muscle except one—and then to be able to fire that one off at will. This feat, of course, is much more precise than any usually required in EMG biofeedback training to control muscle tension levels.

Tension Headache

The pain of a tension headache (muscular-contraction headache is a more accurate description) results from the continued contraction of neck and scalp muscles. If individuals could be taught to relax these muscles, would the pain go away? Two researchers at the University of Colorado Medical School, Thomas Budzynski and Johann Stoyva, thought that the answer might be Yes. They were the first, to our knowledge, to use EMG biofeedback training for tension headaches.[2]

We'd like to describe one of their studies briefly.[3] After careful screening, they chose eighteen persons who had histories of severe tension headaches over a period of several years. All eighteen kept records of the severity of their headaches for each waking hour of each day for two weeks before beginning any biofeedback training. Then they continued keeping such records during training and for three months afterward.

After the initial two weeks of record-keeping, all eighteen were assigned to one of three groups. Group A received EMG training; Group B received pseudotraining (the EMG feedback signals they heard were recordings of subjects in Group A); and Group C received no training but kept daily records of headaches.

Groups A and B did thirty minutes of EMG training twice a week for eight weeks, a total of sixteen sessions. In addition, they were told to practice on their own twice a day for fifteen to twenty minutes without any EMG instruments. All three groups were followed for three months after the sixteen training sessions.

The individuals in Group A (true EMG training) averaged significantly lower forehead tension levels, and significantly less headache activity, and they dramatically decreased the medications they used. Four of the six persons in Group A showed significant decreases in headaches, only one of six in Group B (pseudotraining) showed any significant reduction, and none of those in Group C (no training) showed any significant decrease in headache levels.

This study also demonstrated the importance of regular daily practice at home. For example, the two subjects in Group A who did not show significant improvement also reported difficulty in finding time to do the relaxation practice at home. We would like to emphasize the importance of *regular practice in addition to training with biofeedback instruments.* This is crucial to successful biofeedback training. After all, a person spends many *years* learning how to respond to daily experiences in ways that result in tension headaches (or other stress problems). Thus, it takes considerable practice to learn (in *weeks*) how to react so as not to bring on a headache.

The subjects in this study progressed through a sequence that is typical in biofeedback training. A first stage is increased awareness of tension (which may even seem to be worse, though it isn't) with little ability to decrease it. This increased awareness can be frustrating but it is necessary for progress. This stage is followed by stages of increasing ability to remove the tension (and get rid of accompanying mild to moderate headaches).

The crucial learning comes when the trainee starts applying the skill directly to the stressful aspects of his or her life. As this is done, it becomes easier to face stressful events without overreacting. In fact, some trainees find their moderation almost automatic.

The numerous studies of EMG biofeedback training from the forehead area for muscular contraction, or tension, headaches have been reviewed by a special study section of the Biofeedback Society of America.[4] In their conclusions, they state the following (words in parentheses and italics added):

There is little doubt that a frontal (forehead) EMG biofeedback relaxation program combined with *regular relaxation practice outside the clinic* will alleviate or eliminate muscle-contraction (tension) headaches in 70 percent or more of the cases. The remaining 30 percent or less who do not succeed are frequently those with unresolved secondary gains (emotional payoffs as a result of the headaches that they do not want to give up) or other motivational factors. Furthermore, several studies have suggested that the combined or mixed headache case may not respond as favorably to frontal EMG training as would the pure tension headache. Thermal (skin temperature) or BVP (blood volume pulse) from the temporal artery location appears to add to the effectiveness of the EMG biofeedback training for mixed headache conditions.

Anxiety

We've all experienced anxiety on occasion—being apprehensive or worried about what might happen. Fortunately, for most of us anxiety occurs only rarely and then passes. But for about one person in twenty anxiety is a daily occurrence. Estimates are that at least 5 percent of the population of the United States suffers from *chronic* anxiety—apprehension or dread that persists or occurs regularly. The feeling is accompanied by physiological changes, such as increased heart rate, irregular heartbeat, dizziness, nausea, or diarrhea.

Ten persons with persistent anxiety were trained in EMG feedback.[5] These ten had continued to suffer from anxiety symptoms despite two years of treatment with individual psychotherapy and medication. Training to relax deeply by EMG feedback was followed by eight weeks of home practice without instruments, for two half-hour sessions daily. All ten subjects were

---

It's 5:30 P.M. and you've hurried through the supermarket getting the things you need. Then, you pick what seems to be the shortest and quickest checkout line. What happens? Two people in front of you decide to write checks for tiny purchases. By the time they get their identification out and their checks written and approved, what are you doing? This is a good time to let the tensions go from your body, part by part.

able to reach deep levels of relaxation with and without feedback. When periods of very severe anxiety occurred at home, nearly all could interrupt the anxiety with thirty to forty-five minutes of relaxation practice. Four of the ten also showed moderate to marked improvement in managing anxiety symptoms outside the home throughout the day.

In another setting, EMG feedback and relaxation training was more effective than group therapy.[6] The feedback group received nine twenty-minute EMG feedback training sessions in two weeks followed by two weeks of half hour daily practice in muscle relaxation using tape-recorded relaxation instructions (three hours of feedback and five hours of taped relaxation instruction). The comparison group received hour-long psychotherapy sessions in groups of four to five, four days a week for four weeks (16 one-hour sessions). The feedback group registered significant decreases in EMG levels and in scores on tests measuring mood and trait anxiety. No changes occurred for those in group therapy.

The practitioners doing the second study felt that as more is learned about training anxiety-prone individuals, the improvement rate will increase. It does appear that persons having such thoroughly learned anxieties do require intensive biofeedback training—but any form of treatment with them would have to be intensive—and biofeedback is to be preferred over reliance on drugs.

Those interested in a more comprehensive summary of biofeedback training as a potential treatment for anxiety will want to refer to the chapter discussing this in R. J. Gatchel's book, *Clinical Applications of Biofeedback: Appraisal and Status.*[7]

Three psychiatrists had a unique way of using EMG training to help reduce the anxiety tensions of a large number of their patients.[8] This highly original study has not received the attention it deserves, in our opinion. When first referred, each patient was hooked up to a visual display of his muscle tension. Then he was given a tranquilizer to demonstrate the dramatic decrease in muscle tension that is possible with relaxation. After this, he was told that he had to practice relaxation exercises and to learn to control muscle tension without the aid of a tranquilizer before he could see the doctors for psychotherapy. Each week he came back and was hooked up to the visual display to see how his practice was progressing. When he finally learned to relax voluntarily, the psychiatrists said that they now would see him for the anxiety problem. Most subjects said that they no longer needed help—their problems seemed to be going away or perhaps they hadn't been as anxious as they had thought.

Phobias

Many individuals have more specific anxieties, called phobias. Examples are fear of riding in elevators, fear of heights, or fear of public speaking. EMG training is being used in unlearning such fears. A person trains on instruments to learn to relax deeply. Then, while maintaining the deep relaxation, he imagines himself approaching and doing the feared activity—a process called *systematic desensitization*. As he is able to do this and still maintain his relaxation (as measured by the EMG instrument), he then tries the real thing, using the skills he has practiced.

In a gathering of biofeedback clinicians, reports of using this procedure to help persons cure phobias are likely to be heard. These usually are reports of individual cases. More extensive research has been done by Budzynski and Stoyva, who have been using EMG feedback desensitization for more than ten years with many kinds of phobias.[9] One woman in her mid-forties got so anxious at social gatherings that her right hand trembled and she couldn't shake hands or hold a glass. After EMG training and desensitization, she participated in social situations with no sign of the hand tremor. A management consultant developed such a fear of public speaking that he had to turn down lucrative offers to speak. He learned how to overcome his phobia of public speaking. Once in a while he does get a brief relapse of the phobia, but he quickly controls it by using skills learned in his EMG biofeedback training.

Psychosis

Persons with psychotic symptoms (serious personality disorders) have responded to EMG training in one study.[10] Twenty individuals diagnosed as schizophrenic were randomly assigned to one of two groups. One group was given six sessions of EMG training (thirty minutes from the forearm and thirty minutes from the forehead each time). The other group listened to tapes of music (they were told it was "music therapy" and proven valuable). The EMG group could relax their forearms better than the music group, scored more nearly normal on personality tests, and were rated significantly better behaviorally by nurses on the wards—nurses who did not know which individuals had which treatment. Since the research emphasis in biofeedback training has been on stress-related disorders, studies of psychiatric disorders are rare as yet. Studies such as this one and those mentioned earlier with persons having chronic anxieties are encouraging, but are far from conclusive.

OTHER APPLICATIONS OF EMG

Insomnia can be helped by EMG training. In one study of six persons with sleep problems, five learned to go to sleep at will.[11] All had been taking sedatives for years and were able to stop. Brain wave feedback (see Chapter 5) is often used with persons having insomnia. However, many individuals have difficulty with this form of feedback and need to learn from EMG feedback training first.

Millions of people grind their teeth, a condition called bruxism, some so badly that their gums bleed. EMG biofeedback training, especially for the jaw muscles, is helpful for this problem.[12] EMG training for pregnant women has helped reduce the time in labor, the need for pain medication, and the total time the physician is involved.[13] Stutterers have profited from EMG training as have those with cerebral palsy, dysphonia (difficulty in pronouncing speech sounds), asthma, and glaucoma. Addicts going through withdrawal, individuals with writer's cramp, and even dental patients have learned to relax through EMG. EMG training has also shown positive effects (such as increased attention span) with hyperactive children.[14]

EMG feedback has been used successfully with persons having tics (uncontrolled muscle spasms) and blepharospasms (eye tics).[15] As all of the reports are of individual cases rather than with more adequately controlled experimental studies, the results must be considered tentative at this point.

We cannot finish without mentioning neuromuscular re-education—training nerves and muscles damaged by injury, stroke, or some disease. Torticollis, or "wry neck," results when muscles in one side of the neck stay too tense and hold the head twisted to one side—an embarrassing condition that can cause considerable discomfort. EMG training to relax the overly tense muscles (and, sometimes, to develop milder tension in the opposite set of muscles) has been helpful to persons with this disorder. As one study concluded, "There appears to be adequate evidence at this time to support the claim that EMG biofeedback of sternocleidomastoid muscle activity may be highly effective in reducing torticollis symptoms."[16]

Ten persons who had lost normal use of one foot ("foot-drop") because of strokes showed twice as much improvement when EMG training was added to their physical therapy as ten others with the same problem who did not have EMG training as part of their rehabilitation.[17] This form of muscle re-education is being used to help in the treatment of some individuals suffering from spinal cord injuries (resulting in loss of the use of arms, legs, and normal bodily functions), strokes, and muscles spasms of unknown origin.[18] Follow-up studies have shown that biofeedback training for neuromuscular re-education can have lasting effects. For example, twenty of thirty-nine patients treated for paralysis of the arm had retained significant gains three months to three years after treatment.[19] In another study, four of six patients had maintained their treatment gains at five-month to one-year follow-ups.

The Biofeedback Society Task Force on Physical Medicine and Rehabilitation states:

> Against a background where no effective means exist for the treatment of movement disorders—drugs, surgical methods, or physical medicine and rehabilitation techniques—biofeedback offers new hope but no miracles. . . . We predict that EMG feedback techniques will become routinely used. The basic usefulness of EMG for patient evaluation, treatment planning, progress testing, and general motivation alone make it a valuable clinical tool. However, EMG feedback techniques will not replace, but rather will add to, the array of existing clinical tools.[20]

New ways in which EMG biofeedback training can be used are being reported each year at the Annual Meeting of the Biofeedback Society of America. EMG training and ST training appear to be the most versatile modes of biofeedback at present.

Notes

1 J. V. Basmajian, "Control and Training of Individual Motor Units," *Science*, 1963, Vol. 141, pp. 440–441.

2 T. H. Budzynski, J. M. Stoyva, and C. S. Adler, "Feedback-Induced Muscle Relaxation: Application to Tension Headaches," *Behavior Therapy and Experimental Psychiatry*, 1970, Vol. 1, pp. 205–211.

3 T. H. Budzunski, J. M. Stoyva, C. S. Adler, and D. J. Mullaney, "EMG Biofeedback and Tension Headache: A Controlled Study," *Psychosomatic Medicine*, 1973, Vol. 35, pp. 484–496. Also a chapter in L. Birk, ed., *Biofeedback: Behavioral Medicine* (New York: Grune and Stratton, 1973).

4 T. Budzynski, "Biofeedback in the Treatment of Muscle-Contraction (Tension) Headache" (Task Force Report of the Biofeedback Society of America), *Biofeedback and Self-Regulation*, 1978, Vol. 3, pp 409-434.

5 M. Raskin, G. Johnson, and T. Rondestvedt, "Chronic Anxiety Treated by Feedback-Induced Muscle Relaxation," *Archives of General Psychiatry*, 1973, Vol. 28, pp. 263–266.

6 R. E. Townsend, J. F. House, and D. Addario, "A Comparison of EMG Feedback and Progressive Muscle Relaxation Training in Anxiety Neuroses," *American Journal of Psychiatry*, 1975, Vol. 132, pp. 598–601.

7 R. J. Gatchel, "Biofeedback and the Treatment of Fear and Anxiety," chapter in R. J. Gatchel and K. P. Price, *Clinical Applications of Biofeedback: Appraisal and Status* (New York: Pergamon Press, 1979).

8 G. Haugen, H. Dixon, and H. Dickel, *A Therapy for Anxiety Tension Reactions* (New York: Macmillan, 1963).

9 T. Budzynski and J. Stoyva, "Biofeedback Techniques in Behavior Therapy," reprinted in D. Shapiro and others, eds., *Biofeedback and Self-Control, 1972* (Chicago: Aldine, 1973).

10 A. Nigl, B. Jackson, and G. Murphy, "EMG Biofeedback and Relaxation as Adjunctive Treatment Modalities for Acute Schizophrenia," *Proceedings of the Biofeedback Society of America, 1980* (Denver: Biofeedback Society of America, 1980).

11 Raskin, Johnson, and Rondestvedt, cited in note 5.

12 W. K. Solberg and J. D. Rugh, "The Use of Biofeedback Devices in the Treatment of Bruxism," *Southern California Dental Association Journal*, 1972, Vol. 40, pp. 852–853.

13 R. H. Gregg, L. M. Frazier, and R. A. Nesbit, "Effects of Techniques of Biofeedback on Relaxation during Childbirth," *Proceedings of the Biofeedback Research Society, 1976* (Denver: Biofeedback Research Society, 1976).

14 B. Guitar, "Reduction of Stuttering Frequency Using Analog Electromyographic Feedback," *Journal of Speech and Hearing Research*, 1975, Vol. 18, pp. 672–685. R. I. Lanyon, "Effect of Biofeedback on Stuttering During Reading and Spontaneous Speech," *Journal of Consulting and Clinical Psychology*, 1977, Vol. 5, pp. 860–866. W. W. Finley, C. Niman, J. Standley, and P. Ender, "Frontal EMG Biofeedback Training of Athetoid Cerebral Palsy Patients: A Report of Six Cases," *Biofeedback and Self-Regulation*, 1976, Vol. 1, pp. 169–182. B. L. Bird and others, "Generalization of EMG Biofeedback in Choreoathetoid Cerebral Palsy," *Proceedings of the Biofeedback Society of America, 1979.* K. O. Lyndes, "Application of Biofeedback to Functional Dysphonia," *Proceedings of the Biofeedback Research Society, 1975.* H. Kotes and others, "Muscle Relaxation Effects on Peak Expiration Flow Rate in Asthmatic Children," *Proceedings of the Biofeedback Society of America, 1977.* K. L. Russ, M. Kass, and M. F. O'Connell, "EMG Biofeedback Applied to Patients with Elevated Intraocular Pressure: A Yoked-Control Study Emphasizing Double-Blind Methodology," *Proceedings of the Biofeedback Society of America, 1978.* C. G. Amenhauser and R. Shipley, Jr. "EMG and Its Effect on Withdrawal," *Proceedings of the Biofeedback Society of America, 1977.* M. Crabtree and T. Atmore, "Effects of Biofeedback and Relaxation Training on Anxiety in Recovering Alcoholics and Drug Addicts." *Proceedings of the Biofeedback Society of America, 1980.* C. S. Leeb, "Treatment of a Case of Writer's Cramp Using EMG Biofeedback," *Proceedings of the Biofeedback Society of America, 1980.* M. P. Miller, P. J. Murphy, T. P. Miller, and A. D. Smouse, "The Effects of EMG Feedback and Progressive Relaxation Training on Stress Reactions in Dental Patients," *Proceedings of the Biofeedback Research Society, 1976.* L. W. Braud, "The Effects of Frontal EMG Biofeedback and Progressive Relaxation upon Hyperactivity and its Behavioral Concomitants," *Biofeedback and Self-Regulation*, 1978, Vol. 3, pp. 67–89. R. T. Linn and J. K. Hodge, "Use of EMG Biofeedback Training in Increasing Attention Span and Internalizing Locus of Control in Hyperactive Children," *Proceedings of the Biofeedback Society of America, 1980.*

15 S. S. Fotopoulos and W. P. Sunderland, "Biofeedback in the Treatment of Psychophysiologic Disorders" (Task Force Report of the Biofeedback Society of America), *Biofeedback and Self-Regulation*, 1978, Vol. 3, pp. 331–361.

16 *Ibid.*, p. 336.

17 J. V. Basmajian, C. G. Kukulka, J. C. Narayan, and K. Takebe, "Biofeedback Treatment of Foot-Drop After Stroke Compared with Standard Rehabilitation Technique: Effects on Voluntary Control and Strength," *Archives of Physical Medicine and Rehabilitation*, 1975, Vol. 56, pp. 231–236.

18 J. V. Basmajian and J. P. Hatch, "Biofeedback and the Modification of Skeletal Muscular Dysfunctions," chapter in R. J. Gatchel and K. P. Price, eds., *Clinical Applications of Biofeedback: Appraisal and Status* (New York: Pergamon Press, 1979).

19 J. Brudney and others, "EMG Feedback Therapy: Review of Treatment of 114 Patients," *Archives of Physical Medicine and Rehabilitation*, 1976, Vol. 57, pp. 55-61.

20 C. K. Fernando and J. V. Basmajian, "Biofeedback in Physical Medicine and Rehabilitation" (Task Force Report of the Biofeedback Society of America), *Biofeedback and Self-Regulation*, 1978, Vol. 3, pp. 435-455; quotation is from p. 448.

5

EEG: BRAIN WAVE BIOFEEDBACK TRAINING

So far we have described skin temperature feedback (ST), which is associated with blood flow, and electromyographic training (EMG), for control of muscles. Those seeking biofeedback training for help with the sorts of stress-related disorders discussed in Chapter 2 will probably be doing these forms of training since they have been found to be helpful and efficient in regulating the symptoms of stress.

In this chapter we will introduce a third major form of biofeedback— electroencephalographic (EEG) training, commonly called brain wave training. Tiny electrical impulses from billions of brain cells, which carry small electrical charges, can be detected by electrodes placed on the scalp and connected to an EEG instrument. These impulses, or brain waves, were discovered in 1924 by Hans Berger, a German researcher. Since then it has been estimated that more than a million miles of pen-and-ink records of brain waves have been gathered, nearly all in attempts to find relationships between particular brain wave frequencies and our thought processes, behavior patterns, or illnesses.[1]

One reason this extensive record of brain wave patterns has not resulted in more knowledge is the difficulty in relating a brain function to a mental activity when the electrical activity of the brain is a continuously changing pattern. EEG biofeedback training can provide a person with the ability to produce relatively "steady states."[2] Sustaining steady patterns of brain activity makes it easier to describe the accompanying mental activity and associated emotions and feelings. It becomes possible to produce and sustain brain states conducive to learning new material, concentration, recall, creativity, or correcting the consequences of irregular brain functions such as epilepsy.

EEG patterns are complex and difficult to define. Yet, as a leading researcher in the field has stated, "Even in the relatively early stage of development of EEG biofeedback there is adequate rationale for exploring and using various kinds of EEG biofeedback."[3]

Thirty-four years after Hans Berger's discovery of brain waves, research psychologist Joe Kamiya discovered that individuals could produce different brain wave patterns at will.[4] He wondered if people could control a particular range of brain wave frequencies called alpha rhythms. He attached electrodes to his subjects on the scalp at the back of the head. Each time a bell rang, they were to guess whether they were in brain wave state A (alpha) or brain wave state B (beta), a faster brain wave rhythm. They were told if they were correct. By the second hour, Kamiya's subjects were correct about 60 percent of the time, and by the third hour 75 to 80 percent correct. Some individuals became so sensitive that they were correct 100 percent of the time.

Then Kamiya discovered that his subjects could produce the alpha and beta brain waves on command. When a bell was rung twice, they could enter state A; when the bell was rung once, they could switch to state B, and back and forth.

Another researcher, Barbara Brown, has worked with lights and brain waves.[5] She has designed equipment so that when a particular brain wave pattern appears a colored light comes on. Subjects were able to discover how to operate the lights—how to change their internal states to control the brain waves.

These weak electrical impulses, detected by electrodes on the scalp, are measured by an electroencephalograph (EEG). The strength of the EEG signal (its amplitude) is measured in microvolts. It also varies in frequency, or cycles per second.

BRAIN WAVE RHYTHMS

Four brain wave patterns (called rhythms) have been generally accepted by researchers in electroencephalography. These are shown in Figure 8. Though there are disagreements over the exact limits of each of these rhythms, the ranges described below are most widely agreed upon.

These rhythms are identified by the number of times the electrical signals oscillate each second, that is, their cycles per second, or Hertz (abbre-

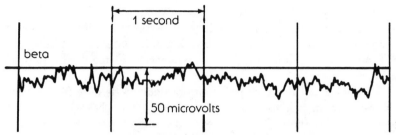

This EEG record of beta waves was taken from an electrode on the scalp at the back of the head. Beta waves are fast—from 13 to 40 cycles per second and higher—and have small amplitude.

Alpha waves, 8 to 13 cycles per second, are often symmetrical, with large amplitude.

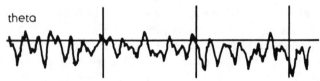

Theta waves, 4 to 8 cycles per second, are less regular, with lower amplitude than alpha waves.

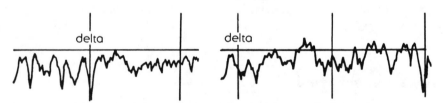

Delta waves, 0.5 to 4 cycles per second, are irregular. The first strip shows theta followed by a large delta wave, with several delta waves in the second tracing.

Figure 8 *Typical EEG Patterns*

viated Hz). All rhythms are usually present to some degree, with the conditions described below determining which one predominates.

Beta Rhythm

This is the rhythm that predominates when you are mentally aroused. It is associated with being awake, alert, active, focusing outside yourself, doing concrete problem-solving or being anxious. Beta is the major rhythm when you are attentively looking at and listening to a speaker or a television program.

Alpha Rhythm

This was the first rhythm to be identified in the EEG because of its obvious pattern; note how symmetrical it appears in the sample EEG recording. The amount of alpha increases in most individuals when they close their eyes and their bodies are relaxed. However, up to perhaps 10 percent of all individuals produce virtually no alpha when they close their eyes while about an equal percentage seem to produce nearly constant alpha with eyes open or closed. This rhythm is associated with putting your mind in neutral so that there is not much mental activity going on. Some persons report enjoying this sort of mindless state (perhaps because it is a welcome break from an overly busy mind) while others find it boring.

   If you close your eyes while listening to a lecture or watching television and feel somewhat bored, alpha may become the dominant rhythm in you brain wave patterns.

Theta Rhythm

The percentage of theta increases as you become drowsy and are slipping closer to sleep. Perhaps you recall having little "mini-dreams" just before dropping off to sleep. These are often accompanied by increasing theta production. Learning to sustain states associated with increased brain wave production in the alpha-theta border region is sometimes associated with creative insight.

Delta Rhythm

These patterns appear as you drop off into deep and usually dreamless sleep—your lowest mental arousal level. As you move into the dreaming phases of a night's sleep, you produce faster brain waves and your rhythms become similar to that of a wakened state.

To sum up, the brain wave rhythms become slower as a person moves from being outwardly alert or active (beta) to more relaxed and internally focused, (alpha), to drowsy and dropping off to sleep (theta), to deep sleep (delta). However, during sleep when a person is dreaming, the brain wave patterns look more like beta, the pattern characteristic of a person who is awake.

INSTRUMENTS FOR EEG TRAINING

Because brain-wave impulses are electrically very weak (usually about 10 to 75 microvolts) care must be taken in preparing and placing the electrodes so that the impulses can be detected accurately. The scalp is cleaned well and an electrolytic paste is placed on the electrodes to conduct the electrical impulses to the recording instrument.

Special care is needed in designing and building EEG instruments. The electrical impulses are weak, and because eye movements can look like brain wave patterns in the EEG, these must be carefully filtered out. Furthermore, usually some combination of the various brain wave frequencies appears at the same time in a person's EEG, requiring especially well-made filters to feed back only the presence of the particular brain wave pattern being trained. A good EEG biofeedback instrument costs from $600 to several thousand dollars. There are some inexpensive (and generally inaccurate) instruments on the market sold usually by non-biofeedback companies. These should be avoided, unless one is especially knowledgeable about EEG feedback instrumentation and training. As we shall have occasion to mention later, inaccurate instruments can lead to training something other than brain waves, without one's being aware that such is happening.

The feedback usually is by a tone which signals that the brain wave being trained is present on the EEG.

WIRING UP AND TRAINING

The typical EEG biofeedback instrument has three electrodes that are placed on the head. In one arrangement one electrode is placed on the back of the head just up from the base of the skull and the other two are attached to the earlobes. The back of the head position is over the occipital lobes of the brain, an area associated with vision and imagery. Training from this arrangement can increase awareness of mental imagery and enhance the ability to control this aspect of our mental activity.

Another placement may focus on the forehead or frontal area of the skull. This area of the brain is sometimes referred to as the association area and seems important in integrating mental activity. Training from this arrangement may help increase awareness of and ability to regulate the stream of ideas and thoughts continually flowing through our minds.

A third location for electrode placement is over the sensory and motor areas on the side of the scalp toward the midline of the brain. As will be seen later in this chapter, biofeedback from this area has been explored as a possible way of learning to control epileptic seizures. These are just three of the many configurations of electrode placements that are used in EEG biofeedback training.

Before attaching the electrodes, the locations to be used on the scalp or ears are cleaned with alcohol or some slightly gritty paste. A special conducting paste is placed on the electrodes and they are secured in place, usually by elastic bands.

The physical setting for training varies. Some trainers use very quiet rooms with low lights and just one person training at a time. One of the authors (Danskin) uses a well-lighted and somewhat noisy room, often with several people training at a time. He feels this helps a person generalize the training to everyday situations more easily; however, it also makes the initial training more difficult for persons who are easily distracted.

Each training session usually is no longer than an hour. The trainee normally is left alone a portion of the time since external interruptions can impede progress, especially at the beginning of training. Most, if not all, of the first training session may be spent explaining the process and demonstrating how the instruments work. Such explanation seems to help in subsequent biofeedback training.

It is extremely important to train with an experienced professional. There are a number of medical, instrumental, and psychological reasons for this which will be explained in more detail later. Also be sure to consult with your own physician before beginning EEG—or any biofeedback training—if you are seeking to relieve a medical problem. Or, if you are going to train to relieve psychological problems consult with your psychotherapist before beginning any form of biofeedback training. Even a professional trainer is unqualified to judge a medical condition or psychological condition if that person is not a physician or mental health professional.

The goal of most EEG training is to increase the production of certain brainwave patterns, usually alpha, theta, or beta. There are some exceptions, such as in training individuals with epilepsy, in which the goal often is decreasing the presence of a particular pattern. With either goal, the emphasis is on developing conscious awareness of the internal subjective experiences (thoughts, feelings, locus of attention) and states associated with the feedback for the various brain waves.

Training involves the same passive concentration that was described for EMG training—letting it happen rather than forcing it to happen. Usually, no relaxation exercises are read to the subject or played on a tape. Such external distractions interfere with the brain wave training and, in most trainees, result in focusing outside themselves, which produces a preponderance of beta patterns in the EEG.

Imagery and *passive* visualization play important roles in the strategies most individuals use, as does breathing. Focusing on a physical function is a favorite strategy—feeling the cool air pass in through the nostrils and the warm air pass out, or feeling one's pulse throbbing in a finger or in some part of the body. Some individuals find an effective strategy something they describe as "listening to the sounds of silence." Others focus on some sort of a void, such as an empty blue sky with an occasional cloud drifting across it.

During the training, one helpful strategy is to let things run freely through the mind, and not to think about them or interact with them. This is hard to do, as most of us "chase after" the ideas that come into our heads. But, with practice, one can learn to be a passive observer and just be aware of what is going on. What might be going on could be meaningless or important, silly or serious. Whatever, the trainee should be patient in learning to do EEG training, and enjoy it.

THE HERITAGE OF EEG

The practice of willful changes in internal states has been part of some religions for thousands of years. Development of EEG instruments has made it possible to measure more precisely just how much voluntary control can be learned. For example, brain wave records have been made of persons practicing a yoga form of meditation.[6] When adept practitioners were deep into their meditative state, their EEG records showed a steady abundance of theta waves. Ordinarily, theta appears when a person is dropping off to sleep; with the actual onset of sleep slower delta waves then appear in abundance. However, individuals practicing yoga meditation were able to sustain the theta state. In fact, even when gongs were sounded near them, lights flashed in their eyes, or a hot test tube pressed on their skin, there was no shift in their theta rhythms. A person who was merely sleeping or on the edge of sleep would be aroused by these intrusions and the brain wave patterns would shift and be dominated by beta rhythms. Thus, these yoga adepts were clearly demonstrating learned voluntary control of psychological and physiological processes.

Japanese monks practicing *zazen*, a form of Zen Buddhist meditation, also demonstrated this voluntary self-regulation of psychophysiological processes. When into *zazen*, they were able to demonstrate a predictable controlled sequence, beginning with mostly alpha, then slower alpha, with bursts of theta in the EEGs of the most accomplished meditators.[7]

In both these examples voluntary control of mental activity is apparent. Willful control of an individual's focus of attention has much to do with what that individual *wants to have happen*. EEG biofeedback may well help individuals learn to voluntarily direct their focus of attention in order to enhance the psychological states associated with the various brain wave rhythms.

Swami Rama, an adept Indian yogi, gave some demonstrations of remarkable regulation of brain wave patterns in a research laboratory at the Menninger Foundation.[8] At first, he experimented to find out the relationships between the inner states of awareness he had learned in India and the tones representing the various brain wave patterns. When he understood these, he could show dramatic changes in his EEG patterns in just a few minutes. While thinking about an empty blue sky, he produced 70 percent alpha patterns. Next, he produced 75 percent theta patterns, which he described as "stilling the conscious mind and bringing forward the unconscious."

Then one day, after being wired up to the instruments, he meditated for five minutes, lay down, shut his eyes, and began producing delta waves (usually seen only in deep sleep) while snoring gently. During the twenty-five minutes he did this, Alyce Green spoke four sentences about five minutes apart, without having told Swami Rama ahead of time that she was going to do so. At the end of the twenty-five minutes, the Swami roused himself, repeated three and a half of the four sentences word for word (and got the gist of the remaining half sentence correct); he remarked that two doors had been slammed shut someplace in the building during the time, and commented on the clicking sounds caused by someone with hard heels walking on the floor above.

This is a paradoxical situation—delta waves in the EEG usually indicate sleep and unconsciousness of what is going on around one. Yet Swami Rama was able to monitor his consciousness even when sleep-related brain waves were present, a dramatic demonstration. It took years for him to learn this skill. However, it seems possible that attaching an EEG instrument could facilitate learning the self-awareness and focusing of attention necessary to influence the psychophysiological processes associated with sleep. Such self-regulation could be a move toward influencing our waking and sleep cycles. Self-reports of persons doing alpha-theta training support this potential—for example, reports of needing less sleep at night and waking refreshed in the morning. It should be stressed, however, that such self-reports have not yet been corroborated by controlled scientific testing.

Brain wave patterns have no sensations we can use to detect their presence or absence. Individuals can feel the difference between tensed and relaxed muscles or feel their hands get warmer as they do ST feedback training, but we do not feel brain waves. Rather, we learn increased awareness (and control) of internal thoughts, feelings, points of attention, and states. These are what we willfully change and which result in varying brain wave patterns. Of course, this actually is how we do all biofeedback training—by imagining muscles letting go, hands getting warmed, or whatever our particular strategies and awareness happen to be.

Brain wave training, of all the types of biofeedback, has been the most sensationalized and most capitalized on by hucksters and opportunists. All sorts of claims have been made by such individuals, who have often perverted and distorted this legitimate form of biofeedback. Alpha waves, especially, have received inordinate attention. This brain wave state has been touted as bliss, a cure for nearly all diseases, the source for great ideas, and even a state for being telepathic.

But the Indian Swami Rama probably gave the most accurate description of alpha. After visualizing an empty blue sky and producing almost constant alpha, he told the researchers, "I have news for you, alpha isn't everything. It is literally nothing." And, this is true. Were everyone in the United States to get wired to an EEG, about 90 percent would show some increase in alpha just by closing their eyes, and could learn how to show more alpha by turning inward and slowing down their thinking or focusing on nothing.

But perhaps the fact that alpha "is nothing" gives a clue to its popularity. Most of us are unable to sustain such a state of nothingness—our minds are going all the time, with beta dominating (unless we are going to sleep). So it feels refreshing to have some periods of nothing—and it feels even better to practice EEG feedback and learn to increase our alpha production.

This is supported by the reports of subjective experiences of most persons doing alpha training. They report such things as feeling more peaceful, more detached from what is going on around them, and just comfortably passive and more at ease. (A few report alpha as being boring.)

Such reports have encouraged some biofeedback trainers to use EEG training for helping persons with general feelings of anxiety. When EEG training is used to help individuals learn how to overcome anxiety, the reported results are mixed—some are helped, others aren't. This application of EEG training is still being explored. EMG or ST training is more frequently used to help persons with anxieties.

APPLICATIONS OF EEG FOR
BEHAVIORAL AND PHYSICAL DISORDERS

We'd like to make two points before discussing EEG training further. First, most brain wave research has tried only to find particular EEG patterns associated with particular behaviors. Much less has been done about finding applications for it or using EEG as a treatment than has been done with some of the other forms of biofeedback. For example, typical EEG research has looked at the EEG in relation to emotions, use of drugs, aging, physical or mental disorders, meditation, or reports of subjective states. But relatively few studies have examined the actual effects of EEG training on such factors.

Second, there continues to be both fascination with EEG training and interest in its potential for treatment of both physical and psychological disorders.

The treatment of epilepsy is one of the applications of EEG training receiving considerable attention. It results from some rather fortuitous circumstances. Physiologist Maurice B. Sterman had taught cats to increase the percentage from one location on the head of a particular segment of the EEG—12 to 16 cycles per second—called the *sensorimotor rhythm* (SMR). The cats learned to do this after being given some milk each time their brains produced SMR.

Shortly after this experiment, Sterman had to test some rocket fuels to see how toxic they might be to humans. He did not have enough cats for the new experiment, so he also used those from the SMR training study. Sterman noted that the SMR-trained cats did not develop convulsions at concentrations of rocket fuel normally inducing seizures in the other cats. This led him to wonder if seizures in humans with epilepsy could be decreased by means of SMR training. His initial work was encouraging; he and a number of others are continuing to study this form of EEG training for epilepsy.

Electrodes for detecting the SMR rhythm are placed above the ears toward the top of the head. The amplitude of the SMR is of very low voltage and requires special electronic filters to be isolated and identified. One feedback display uses rows of lights to show increases in the amounts of SMR produced. Another ingenious system employs a projector displaying progress in completing a picture puzzle as progress in producing more SMR is made. Results suggest that many, but not all, individuals with epilepsy are helped through this form of training. Reductions in seizures of 50 percent or more in about half of epileptics trained in research labs seem to be about average.[9] There are a number of major controversies in the field, because there are different types of epilepsy and the part of the brain exhibiting abnormal EEG patterns varies. For a recent summary of research in this area, see Kuhlman and Kaplan.[10]

Another form of EEG feedback training used with epileptics, but not studied systematically as yet, focuses on beta and alpha enhancement. Seizures are usually accompanied by an increase in slower, larger amplitude rhythms. Thus, if the training is to enhance the faster, lower amplitude (beta) frequencies, the onset of a seizure can be aborted by reproducing the state associated with enhanced beta. Training to learn to distinguish states associated with alpha from states associated with beta gives this awareness and control.

Alpha brain wave biofeedback training may prove of special value in reducing excessive mental activity and obsessions. Some persons become so obsessed with their peculiar thoughts and rituals as to let them interfere with normal healthy activity.

Five persons with a history of obsessions, who had not been helped by psychotherapy, were trained in EEG alpha feedback.[11] Their obsessions had been very resistant to treatment. One subject compulsively had to wash her hands over and over for fear of contamination. Another, when seeing an object such as an ashtray out of place, had to touch the object, snap his fingers and think "train," the letter "Q," and "flam." These five individuals received twenty biofeedback training sessions to enhance alpha production. Four of the five reported that during training they felt relaxed, daydreamed a lot, and quit thinking. All five showed a diminishment in their obsessions during training—this was the first time these individuals had found relief in any treatment. However, the seeming improvement did not carry over to their regular daily lives. The researchers were encouraged by the diminishment of obsessive thoughts during training, and feel that this approach has promise as more is learned about how to help obsessive individuals transfer the training to daily life.

Perhaps one key is found in a report by two other researchers.[12] They were doing synchronized alpha training, in addition to ST training, with a person suffering from headaches that had been resistant to treatment. This person also was obsessive and compulsive, like those just described. Synchronized alpha is training for predominant alpha in the EEG from both hemispheres of the brain at the same time. In this study, such training was successful in reducing the obsessive behavior as well as the headaches.

The effects of EEG training on hyperkinetic children to increase SMR is being studied by Joel Lubar at the University of Tennessee.[13] Hyperkinetic children have extremely short attention spans and do not pay attention long enough to complete most tasks. Also, they are overactive and "all over the place" much of the time. Hence, they can be very distracting in a classroom or at home. Lubar is showing that EEG training to increase the presence of 12 to 14 cycles per second of brain wave activity is more effective than medication (Ritalin) for most of the children he is training, especially when overactivity rather than distractibility is the dominant hyperkinetic behavior.

Earlier in this chapter we mentioned that as a person goes to sleep, slower brain wave frequencies predominate. This suggests that EEG training to learn to increase the presence of brain waves in the slow alpha to theta range might help insomniacs. However, results thus far are mixed.

Anxiety is another area of EEG research. In one study, practice at increasing and decreasing alpha activity resulted in lower anxiety for persons with general anxiety feelings.[14]

Seven individuals suffering from anxiety took a personality test twice, had 48-minute alpha feedback training sessions each day for seven days, and then retook the same test. Comparing changes on the test and EEG changes from several different locations on the skull suggests that specific EEG locations might be related to specific personality characteristics—and these vary among locations.[15] This suggests the need to "map" these relationships, which has not yet been done.

Five persons in a mental hospital were given ten alpha training sessions by Cecil Childers, a psychiatrist at a medical school in San Antonio. All were there because of social behavior problems—they were verbally abusive to others, impulsive, and generally socially obnoxious. After training, there were dramatic improvements in their behavior; all were released in two to three weeks, and some found jobs immediately. Follow-up of them is encouraging.[16] These outcomes are exceptionally good. More typical would be improvement in some individuals but not all.

APPLICATIONS OF EEG
FOR CREATIVITY AND LEARNING

Two other applications of EEG training are receiving increasing attention—to enhance creativity and to improve learning. No chapter on EEG feedback would be complete without mentioning the tantalizing research on creativity by Elmer and Alyce Green and their associate Dale Walters. Highly creative individuals seem to get insights and solutions to problems from images that appear spontaneously in a state of reverie just short of sleep. Preliminary work in the Greens' laboratory suggested to them that these same sorts of images sometimes appeared to a person when theta patterns were present in the EEG.

Volunteers practiced daily for ten weeks at alpha and especially theta training. All kept detailed records and were interviewed frequently. In addition, they regularly came to the main laboratory and did their training. Whenever a burst of theta appeared on the recording paper they were gently asked about what was occurring in their mind at that time.

There were many self-reports of feeling generally better after training sessions, with some individuals saying that they felt somehow intimately connected with what they "wanted to have happen." Reports also mentioned greater ease in taking exams, improved relationships with parents, being able to put ideas together more easily, and the appearance of meaningful symbols in the mental images that came during training.

Twilight learning, so labeled by Budzynski, is just beginning to receive the attention of some EEG researchers. Budzynski felt that several lines of research suggested the potentials for low arousal or "twilight" state, which is similar to what the Greens call reverie.[17] He proposed that if a person could learn to maintain this drowsy state without falling asleep, it would be possible to retain information presented, be it foreign language lessons or suggestions for personality change.

Budzynski and his colleagues first use EMG training from the frontal area of the brain to teach low arousal states. Then, they switch to training on a device called a Twilight Learner, which helps the trainee learn to sustain a pattern of theta brain waves. The Twilight Learner is designed so that a cassette recorder automatically turns on and stays on as long as theta waves are produced. If the brain wave pattern changes to alpha, the recorder shuts off. If the frequencies show slower theta waves, indicating movement toward sleep, the volume of the tape recorder is increased, gently nudging the trainee back into the twilight state.

Budzynski reports using this training for many kinds of learning.[18] One example was with a student with a mental block for learning Spanish, who was so anxious he could not study the subject. A tape was made in Spanish and English suggesting that the person would be able to study effectively and remember the material. After training with the tape twelve times, he was able to study and passed his exam easily. In another example, a man had trouble saying no and asserting himself, behavior he tied to an early experience with his father. The trainee reported that he learned to deal more effectively with authority figures and to be more assertive.

Budzynski also reports on a pilot study with eight persons which was designed to determine how much academic content could be learned in the twilight state. For a total of two hours of "theta time" the subjects listened to a passage about tidepool life. Only one subject improved his test scores significantly. The others were brought back for additional training. By the sixth hour, five of the seven subjects had improved their scores significantly. Two did not improve significantly after five hours of training. One vacillated in and out of theta so rapidly that what was learned was quite disconnected. The other slipped into deeper sleep (increased delta waves).

Budzynski has suggested that the actual procedure of twilight learning is quite complicated. Factors include the different types of material to be learned and the many possible different ways to present the material. The choice of words used in making the tape recording and the intonations used in recording it also appear to be important. Furthermore, achieving and maintaining the twilight state takes much practice, but it is certainly within the realm of possibility that this form of EEG treatment will become valuable at some time in the future.

A number of researchers around the country are regularly studying EEG training and creativity or twilight learning. Although the initial results are promising, progress has been slow—one reason being that research on biofeedback training has had a difficult time getting the support of public and private research funding organizations. However, it appears that interest is growing and that there will be an increase in studying and understanding this area of biofeedback more thoroughly.

There is still a newer development in EEG training—training for synchronous brain waves in different parts of the head. Brain wave patterns from one part of the brain do not generally match patterns from another part—they are "out of phase" or not synchronous. When some people relax, a synchronicity appears in their EEG recorded from different sites on the brain, and this is accompanied by feelings of great calm and control—those who experience it usually say that words cannot describe what it's like. Reports of persons who have learned to get their brain waves "in sync" and reports of practitioners who use synchronous training are generating much interest in using and learning more about this type of EEG training.

THE FUTURE OF EEG BIOFEEDBACK

Virtually all the work in EEG training is in very experimental stages—EEG training for anxiety, insomnia, epilepsy, hyperkinesis, creativity, twilight learning, and synchronicity of brain waves. And there are explorations in areas not mentioned, with others on the horizon. Evidence concerning the value of EEG training is just beginning to come in. Increasing numbers of researchers are now doing the careful and laborious work needed to better understand the ways biofeedback training of brain waves can be of value.

The promise of EEG feedback has waxed and waned—waned mostly because too much was promised too fast by persons not working in EEG labs or experienced in EEG training. Expectations are becoming more realistic now and hopes persist, but time will be required to obtain more definite answers about the potential of EEG training.

Notes

1 E. and A. Green, *Beyond Biofeedback* (New York: Delacorte, 1977).

2 B. B. Brown, *Stress and the Art of Biofeedback* (New York: Harper and Row, 1977).

3 *Stress and the Art of Biofeedback* p. 153.

4 J. Kamiya," Operant Control of the EEG Alpha Rhythm and Some of its Reported Effects on Consciousness," in C. T. Tart, ed., *Altered States of Consciousness* (New York: Wiley, 1969).

5 B. B. Brown, "Recognition of Aspects of Consciousness through Association with EEG Alpha Activity Represented by a Light Signal," *Psychophysiology*, 1970, Vol. 6, pp. 442–452.

6 B. K. Anand, G. S. Chhina, and B. Singh, "Some Aspects of Electroencephalographic Studies in Yogis," *Electroencephalography and Clinical Neurophysiology*, 1961, Vol. 13, pp. 452–456.

7 A. Kasamatsu and T. Hirai, "An Electroencephalographic Study of Zen Meditation (Zazen)," *Folia Psychiatrica et Neurological Japonica*, 1966, Vol. 20, pp. 315–336. (The article is in English, for those interested in seeking it out.)

8 E. Green, "Biofeedback for Mind-Body Self-Regulation: Healing and Creativity," in D. Shapiro and others, eds., *Biofeedback and Self-Control, 1972* (Chicago: Aldine, 1973).

9 W. N. Kuhlman, "EEG Feedback Training in the Treatment of Seizures: Mechanisms and Maintenance of Effect," *Proceedings of the Biofeedback Society of America,* 1979 (Denver: Biofeedback Society of America, 1979).

10 W. N. Kuhlman and B. J. Kaplan, "Clinical Applications of EEG Feedback Training," chapter in R. J. Gatchel and K. P. Price, eds., *Clinical Applications of Biofeedback: Appraisal and Status* (New York: Pergamon Press, 1979).

11 G. K. Mills and L. Solyom, "Biofeedback of EEG Alpha in the Treatment of Obsessive Ruminations: An Exploration," *Journal of Behavior Therapy and Experimental Psychiatry*, 1974, Vol. 5, pp. 37–41.

12 M. Wargen and S. L. Fahrion, "A Case Study: Synchronized Alpha Training for the Obsessive-Compulsive Headache Patient," *Biofeedback and Self-Regulation*, 1977, Vol. 2, p. 299.

13 M. N. Shouse and J. F. Lubar, "Operant Conditioning of EEG Rhythms and Ritalin in the Treatment of Hyperkinesis," *Biofeedback and Self-Regulation*, 1979, Vol. 4, pp. 299–312.

14 J. V. Hardt and J. Kamiya, "Anxiety Change through Electroencephalographic Alpha Feedback Seen Only in High Anxiety Subjects," *Science*, 1978, Vol. 201, pp. 79–81.

15 J. V. Hardt, "Personality Change through Voluntary Control of EEG Alpha Activity," *Proceedings of the Biofeedback Society of America, 1978.*

16 C. A. Childers, "Modification of Social Behavior Problems by Alpha Biofeedback Training," *Proceedings of the Biofeedback Research Society, 1975* (Denver: Biofeedback Research Society, 1975).

17 T. H. Budzynski, "Some Applications of Biofeedback Produced Twilight States," *Fields Within Fields . . . Within Fields,* 1972, Vol. 5, pp. 105–114 (The World Institute Council). Reprinted in D. Shapiro and others, eds., *Biofeedback and Self-Control, 1972.*

18 T. Budzynski, "Tuning in on the Twilight Zone," *Psychology Today,* 1977, Vol. 11, pp. 38–44. Also T. Budzynski, "Biofeedback and the Twilight States of Consciousness," in G. E. Schwartz and D. Shapiro, eds., *Consciousness and Self-Regulation: Advances in Research and Theory, Vol. I* (New York: Plenum, 1976).

6

OTHER FORMS OF
BIOFEEDBACK
TRAINING

Thus far we have discussed the three main types of biofeedback training—ST, EMG, and EEG. But other types are being used and deserve to be described. Of these, galvanic skin response, heart rate feedback, and blood pressure feedback are noteworthy. Also, there is a constant search for new forms of biofeedback to be used in training. At present there are a number that have been used very experimentally. We will present some of them briefly as an indication of the wide variety of physiological processes that it may be possible to regulate voluntarily.

Actually, any device or system that gives immediate and ongoing information to an individual about internal biological processes is a biofeedback instrument and the information presented is biofeedback. This definition includes some things that are common to all of us, which will be discussed later in this chapter.

GALVANIC SKIN RESPONSE

How well our skin conducts a tiny electrical current is related to our internal state. This is called the galvanic skin response (GSR), and has been known since the late 1800s. As a person becomes nervous or anxious, perspiration tends to increase, often in minute amounts not noticeable to the eye. This increased moisture heightens the electrical conductance of a tiny electrical current between two points on the skin. As a person relaxes, there is decreased conductance because the skin is dryer.

A GSR biofeedback instrument detects these changes and feeds them back, usually by a tone that wavers up or down as skin conductance changes. If you were attached to a GSR and were startled by someone unexpectedly kicking a wastebasket, the tone probably would increase very noticeably. Or, if you thought of something that made you angry, fearful, or aroused sexual feelings, the tone also would increase. These and other emotions all produce GSR responses, although the specific emotion that elicites the response cannot always be precisely identified.

The actual changes in electrical conductance of the skin, hence changes in GSR feedback, are quite rapid, usually within one or two seconds after meaningful stimulation. Such changes are usually measured from the fingers or the palm of a hand. A number of factors influence the GSR response—taking a deep breath, moving parts of the body, pressure against the electrodes, room temperature and humidity, age, handwashing, or the amount of nicotine and alcohol in the body.[1]

One of the uses of GSR is to demonstrate how the mind and body work together. Attach a friend to a GSR instrument and ask him to think of a number between one and ten but not to tell you. Ask him to keep thinking of the number and to answer "no" each time you ask him the question, "Is it number one?" and so on up through ten. You'll probably be able to guess the number he picked just by listening to the pitch of the GSR feedback instrument. It will have gradually risen in pitch as the number chosen is approached, reaching its highest pitch at the number and then dropping after the number is passed—even though he told you "no" as you mentioned each number. You can see why the GSR is one of the instruments used in lie detector tests!

Such an instrument has also been used to help people overcome phobias. GSR feedback is used in conjunction with desensitization, as described earlier in this book. A person practices learning to keep the GSR feedback tone low and then maintains this low level while imagining approaching closer and closer to the feared object or situation. Learning to control GSR level can also help control general feelings of anxiety.

Because the GSR is sensitive to changes in emotion and thought, some psychologists and psychiatrists use GSR feedback during their regular therapy sessions. They feel it helps them and the person they are counseling to better understand what the important issues really are, as well as helping the person to deal with those issues more calmly.

GSR has been known for a long time, and GSR biofeedback instruments are among the least expensive. But references to GSR biofeedback appear in the literature infrequently, and it appears not to be used as extensively as ST and EMG feedback. One of the reasons it is not used extensively is its sensitivity to the many factors mentioned above.

Although GSR is not used by most biofeedback trainers, or used only in a minor way, the picture may change as biofeedback instrument companies are now developing better instruments for measuring the electrical activity of the skin (electrodermal activity, or EDA). These newer instruments are often called EDA feedback instruments. These are more accurate but also more expensive, which makes them less attractive than cheaper GSR instruments. However, they may be used more frequently in the coming years as skin conductance is better understood.

HEART RATE FEEDBACK

Some heart rate (HR) feedback training uses lights: a small green light indicates an accelerating heart rate, a red light indicates a slowing rate, and a yellow light shows a stable HR. Other systems use a meter or digital display that tells the trainee his HR in beats per minute (BPM). Whatever the system, most are special experimental arrangements not regularly manufactured by biofeedback instrument companies. Again, though, because of advances in technology these biofeedback instruments are beginning to become available to regular practitioners.

A recent survey of the research on learning to control HR lists more than fifty references in the biofeedback literature, making HR the most studied cardiovascular function.[2] A majority of this research has been with persons with normal heart rates to determine if biofeedback helps them learn to speed up or slow down their HR. This research has also been concerned with the effects of types of feedback, length of training, motivation, and other individual differences. More than ten studies have demonstrated average HR increases of greater than 10 BPM. There is great variability between individuals in these studies. For example, in one study, 22 percent had HR increases greater than 20 BPM, another 25 percent had increases greater than 10 BPM, with another 20 percent having increases of only 5 BPM or less.[3] Slowing HR seems more difficult than some other forms of self-regulation.

Bernard Engel has pioneered in the application of HR feedback, working with individuals who have irregular heartbeats, or premature ventricular contractions (PVCs).[4] In PVCs, one heartbeat may follow another almost immediately. When this happens, virtually no blood is pumped by the quick heartbeat because the chamber has not had time to fill with blood between beats. Not getting an adequate supply of fresh blood pumped through the system can be dangerous.

Engel trained persons with PVCs to speed the heart rate, slow the heart rate, alternate speeding and slowing, and maintain the rate within a particular range. Speeding seemed to decrease PVCs for some, slowing did it for others, and maintaining a beat within a range (as between 60 and 70 beats per minute) decreased PVCs for still others. Again nearly all achieved success in the laboratory, but not all were able to transfer the practice to everyday life. In the study referred to here, four of eight persons were still maintaining low PVC rates nearly two years after training.

Some persons show stress through an abnormally fast heart rate, called tachycardia. When the heart rate builds up to 170 or more beats per minute while a person is sitting quietly or even lying in bed, it can be frightening. Heart rate feedback training is one obvious way to learn to control this stress symptom. It is not used very often, however, partly because few practitioners have heart rate biofeedback instruments. Also, stress management training using ST or EMG biofeedback instruments, often in combination with relaxation techniques, seems to be effective with tachycardia.

A unique use of heart rate control training is reported in Chapter 8. Students who very much feared speaking before groups successfully decreased this speech anxiety by learning how to slow their heart rate. Perhaps other such interesting uses will be identified as less expensive heart rate biofeedback instruments become more widely available.

BLOOD PRESSURE FEEDBACK

Remember the last time you had your blood pressure (BP) checked? (It's something you should do regularly.) The nurse or physician put a cuff around your upper arm, pumped air into it, and listened through a stethoscope placed on a blood vessel in your arm. As the air was slowly let out, two numbers were jotted down, such as 126/73. The first and higher number represents systolic pressure in millimeters of mercury (mm Hg), which is the blood pressure as the heart contracts. The second number is the diastolic blood pressure, the pressure between contractions when the heart is momentarily at rest.

This traditional method is too slow and too cumbersome to use in biofeedback training. But cuffs that are controlled automatically are being developed; they automatically inflate and deflate, some as often as every five or six seconds, giving fairly continuous feedback of blood pressure. Continued development will doubtless increase their use.

Research on applications of biofeedback in learning BP control is not as advanced as that for HR, though a recent review by Williamson and Blanchard does list twenty-five references.[5] Most of the studies have been with individuals with hypertension (high BP), with the emphasis on lowering BP. In their summary, Williamson and Blanchard point out the variability among persons in these studies. In one study, 30 to 40 percent of the subjects could consistently reduce systolic BP by as much as 10 mm Hg (i.e., 130 to 120). Three studies have had as many as 55 to 100 percent of the subjects produce such changes. However, yet another study failed to find any subject who could lower BP as much as 5 mm Hg. In examining all the data, the reviewers conclude that some individuals can learn to voluntarily control their BP, with BP lowering more likely than BP increasing. As we learn more about this form of biofeedback training, perhaps more individuals with high BP may be trained in it.

As in any form of biofeedback training, the real significance of the training comes in applying the skill learned to daily life. In BP training, this generalization to daily life is difficult for many. Nonetheless, at least six studies have done short-term follow-ups (a few days or weeks) and all report at least some ability to maintain the self-control learned in the training.[6] However, there are no published studies with one year or more follow-ups.

EXPERIMENTAL FORMS OF BIOFEEDBACK

Biofeedback trainers are an ingenious group, constantly seeking out new forms of feedback. The forms of feedback that follow are still in the experimental stage. We describe them briefly because they suggest that a very wide range of physiological processes may possibly be voluntarily self-regulated. Keep in mind that these techniques are still very experimental. Many of the procedures have been used with just a very few individuals (in some cases only one). Thus, the results, while tantalizing, are only suggestive at this time.

Stethoscope Feedback

We are all familiar with the stethoscope used by doctors and nurses. The modern version is an electronic stethoscope which looks much like the old-fashioned one, but is battery operated and much more sensitive. This fancier instrument has been used in biofeedback training.

One doctor attached an electronic stethoscope to a speaker so that he and his patient could both listen.[7] When the stethoscope is placed over the intestines, gurgling and rumbling sounds can be heard—activity in these organs. This feedback was used with people having functional diarrhea (diarrhea with no apparent physical cause), sometimes more than a dozen attacks in a day, day after day. When the condition is severe, a person cannot hold a job, ride in a car, or engage in ordinary social activities.

Five subjects with functional diarrhea trained themselves to increase and decrease sounds from their own abdomens. All five learned control of the sounds and decreased the number of diarrhea attacks. The most dramatic improvement was in a woman who averaged four to fifteen attacks a day and had been virtually toilet-bound for all of her twenty-four years. She cured herself and now has a job for the first time. When the diarrhea is related to specific fears—such as fear of being trapped in a car away from a toilet— systematic desensitization may also be necessary.

All of these individuals had no other apparent causes for their diarrhea—they had "pure" functional diarrhea. When this is not the case, biofeedback training may take longer and be less successful.

This same sort of feedback shows promise for such related disorders as irritable colons and spastic colons. It also can be used for heart rate training. Some trainees apparently can speed up or slow down their hearts just by listening to the "thump-thump-thump" fed back by the stethoscope. However, people with heart rate problems or with PVCs seem to need more—the lights or digital feedback and the extended practice.

Respiration Feedback

In this form of training for asthmatics, subjects learn to control airway resistance. Bronchial asthma is experienced as labored breathing, with wheezing and tightnesss in the chest. Airway resistance is increased by constriction of the smooth muscles of the bronchioles, the small airway passages leading into the lungs. A biofeedback instrument using a respiratory resistance unit, a polygraph (GSR unit), and a digital computer provide feedback proportional to the resistance in the trainee's respiratory system. So far, however, results of pilot work suggest that this form of feedback by itself has only limited value for asthmatics.[8]

Teaching breathing techniques is used to augment biofeedback training. Many of us tend to have uneven breathing patterns—our exhalations are more rapid than our inhalations. Under stress, breathing from primarily the upper chest (thoracic breathing) is common, as is holding the breath before exhaling. Individuals taught to breathe in and out evenly or to emphasize abdominal breathing report that these techniques help them achieve deeper feelings of relaxation. Most of the respiration research in the biofeedback literature has been on the effects of respiration strategies (such as abdominal breathing), taught *without* using biofeedback instruments, on other physiological functions (heart rate, for example), or on alleviating stress symptoms (high blood pressure). There is very little research that uses instruments feeding back actual breathing patterns.

Two other preliminary studies have been reported on respiration biofeedback training. One study examined the respiratory patterns associated with feelings of happiness and feelings of disgust.[9] Thirty-five women watched films of pleasant scenes and unpleasant ones, and then filled out reports of how they felt. Their faces were also filmed. In addition, abdominal and thoracic respiration were recorded using strain gauges attached to recorders. Analysis was limited to those segments during which the women reported feeling happy and also showed smiles, or where they reported disgust and raised their upper lip. Significant differences in breathing patterns were found. Happy feelings were accompanied by abdominally dominant respiration patterns while feelings of disgust were accompanied by thoracically dominant breathing patterns. To what extent did the breathing patterns affect the subjects' emotional response? At this point we can only speculate on the effects of teaching abdominal versus thoracic breathing.

Another study looked at respiratory changes associated with falling asleep, with the objective of discovering feedback techniques that could be used to enhance the ability of insomniacs to fall asleep.[10] As the participants in the study drifted into the first stage of sleep, there was a shift from relative abdominal dominance in breathing to relative thoracic dominance, with a further shift as the second stage of sleep was approached. Abdominal dominance resumed with waking. As with much of the research reported in this chapter, these studies on respiratory patterns are suggestive of a training strategy but need to be studied much more.

Vapor Pressure Feedback

Most of us have known someone with sweaty hands. Extreme sweating, usually in response to emotional situations, is called *hyperhidrosis*. This profuse sweating can be very embarrassing. A special biofeedback instrument was devised that sensed the amount of vapor pressure or humidity over a patch of skin.[11] The trainee learned to voluntarily dry or wet his hands within one to five minutes in the training laboratory, but could not do it outside the lab. Then, he learned to imagine or fantasize those situations that normally caused excessive sweating, but without actually sweating. This was a desensitization stage of the training. Finally he was able to use his skill outside the lab, to face successfully the formerly sweat-producing situations.

Stomach Acidity Level Feedback

Training to reduce the amount of stomach acid could reduce ulcer activity. Ten persons with duodenal ulcers used a unique feedback system to learn to control the amount of acid secreted into their stomachs.[12] Under controlled laboratory conditions a tube, which is used to test for ulcers, was lowered into the stomach of a patient. From this tube, stomach secretions were frequently pumped to a pH analyzer, which measures acid level. The results were displayed to the trainees so that they could practice changing the pH level in the desired direction.

Using this complicated biofeedback system, there was some decrease in the amount of stomach acid produced. This approach appears promising, but the technique needs to be refined. Where in the stomach the tube is placed is crucial; accurate analysis of pH is important, and difficult to do quickly; and the length of training needed still is unknown.

Sphincter Feedback

Difficulty in controlling bowel movements plagues many adults because of lack of control of the anal sphincter. These people probably can be taught control by an ingenious system. A special balloon is inserted into the rectum, inflated and connected to a pen recorder. The recorder feeds back results of the person's attempts to control the sphincter muscle voluntarily. All of those who tried this improved considerably or learned complete control within two or three practice sessions of an hour each.[13]

Stabilimeter Feedback

Two ingenious researchers placed a stabilimeter feedback platform under hyperactive children's chairs in the classroom.[14] It was wired so that it detected high levels of activity (common in hyperactive children) and provided feedback by a buzzer. Also studied were the effects of a point system (the teacher gave the hyperactive child a "check" for periods of appropriately nonhyperactive behavior) and a combination of the point system and stabilimeter-platform procedure. All three procedures resulted in reductions in hyperactivity levels, with the combined procedure tending to give the greatest reductions.

Blood Chemistry Level Feedback

A new area of biofeedback may well be emerging—measuring and feeding back changes in chemical levels in the body. A number of researchers and instrument companies are working to develop biofeedback systems for monitoring blood sugar or insulin levels, although no formal reports have yet appeared. This form of biofeedback would be a boon to many of the 10 million persons suffering from diabetes, a disorder that is increasing at a rate of 6 percent a year and is a major contributor to heart disease, kidney failure, and blindness.[15] Blood chemistry level feedback could potentially also aid the unknown millions suffering from the fatigue, headaches, and other symptoms of irregular blood sugar levels.

Notes

1 P. H. Venables and M. J. Christie, "Mechanisms, Instrumentation, Recording Techniques and Quantification of Responses," in W. F. Prokasy and D. C. Raskin, eds. *Electrodermal Activity in Psychological Research* (London: Academic Press, 1973).

2 D. A. Williamson and E. B. Blanchard, "Heart Rate and Blood Pressure Biofeedback: I. A Review of the Recent Experimental Literature," *Biofeedback and Self-Regulation,* 1979, Vol. 4, pp. 1–34.

3 J. H. Stephens and others, "Psychological and Physiological Variables Associated with Large Magnitude Voluntary Heart Rate Changes, "*Psychophysiology,* 1975, Vol. 12, pp. 381–387.

4 T. Weiss and B. T. Engel, "Operant Conditioning of Heart Rate in Patients with Premature Ventricular Contractions," *Psychosomatic Medicine,* 1971, Vol. 33, pp. 301–320.

5 D. A. Williamson and E. B. Blanchard, "Heart Rate and Blood Pressure Biofeedback."

6 Ibid.

7 S. Furman, "Intestinal Biofeedback in Functional Diarrhea: A Preliminary Report," *Journal of Behavior and Experimental Psychiatry,* 1973, Vol. 4, pp. 317–321, and in Leo V. DiCara and others, eds., *Biofeedback and Self Control, 1974* (Chicago: Aldine, 1975).

8 R. W. Levenson, S. B. Manuck, H. H. Strupp "A Biofeedback Technique for Bronchial Asthma," *Proceedings of the Biofeedback Research Society* (Denver: Biofeedback Research Society, 1974).

9 S. Ancoli and J. Kamiya, "Respiratory Patterns During Emotional Expression," *Proceedings of the Annual Meeting of the Biofeedback Society,* (Denver: Biofeedback Society of America, 1979).

10 K. Naifeh and J. Kamiya, "Respiratory Changes Associated with Sleep Onset: Implications for Biofeedback," *Proceedings of the 1978 Meeting of the Biofeedback Society,*

(Denver: Biofeedback Society of America, 1978). E. L. Hukill and A. Turner, "Feedback of Respiratory Patterns," *Proceedings of the Biofeedback Research Society,* (Denver: Biofeedback Research Society, 1975).

11 W. H. Rickles, "Treatment of a Case of Hyperhidrosis with Vapor Pressure Feedback," *Proceedings of the 1978 Annual Meeting of the Biofeedback Society* (Denver: Biofeedback Society of America, 1978).

12 K. A. Hubel, "Voluntary Control of Gastrointestinal Function: Operant Conditional and Feedback," *Gastroenterology,* 1974, Vol. 66, pp. 1085–1090, and in Leo V. DiCara and others, eds.) *Biofeedback and Self-Control, 1974.*

13 B. T. Engel, P. Nikopmanesh, and M. M. Schuster, "Operant Conditioning of Recto-sphincteric Responses in the Treatment of Fecal Incontinence," *New England Journal of Medicine,* 1974, Vol. 290, pp. 646–649.

14 P. R. Krasner and S. Phillips, "The Control of Hyperactivity in Neurologically Impaired Children using a Point System and Stabilimeter Feedback," *Proceedings of the Biofeedback Society of America, 1980.*

15 American Diabetes Association, "Facts about Diabetes." Undated, but circulated in 1980.

7

███████████████████

SELECTING
BIOFEEDBACK CENTERS
AND TRAINING

Once you decide you want to take biofeedback training, how do you arrange it? If you live in a large city, your telephone directory may list a biofeedback training center. Chances are, however, that you will have to look further. Biofeedback training programs are usually associated with larger educational or healthcare organizations. Places in which you might find them include headache treatment clinics in hospitals, mental health centers, physical therapy units, college or university counseling centers or psychology departments, offices of health professionals in private practice (such as psychologists, psychiatrists, social workers, counselors), or occasionally in clinics supported by churches. For convenience, we will refer to all biofeedback training centers as BFTCs in this chapter.

The title of the person doing the training will vary—biofeedback clinician, biofeedback therapist, biofeedback counselor, biofeedback technician, or biofeedback trainer. We prefer to use the title "biofeedback trainer" or "trainer." It emphasizes the trainee's active role in biofeedback rather than the more passive role sometimes associated with the clinician, therapist, or doctor.

LOCATING A BIOFEEDBACK TRAINING CENTER

The availability of BFTCs varies unpredictably; some cities have several centers and others of similar size have none. Some regions have many centers

(Kansas, for example, has biofeedback training in mental health centers in a number of small towns), whereas other areas are just developing this service.

The first likely source of information about a biofeedback trainer is your physician. If he doesn't know of one, you can use the Yellow Pages of the phone book and call the offices of the doctors, psychologists, physical therapists, osteopaths, dentists, and chiropractors listed for sources of biofeedback training.

If none of these resources can recommend someone to you, write the Biofeedback Society of America and ask for the name of the president of the biofeedback society for your state. Not all members do training, but the state president may know who does offer training in the region. The address for the society is: Biofeedback Society of America, 4301 Owens Street, Wheat Ridge, CO 80033. Please send a stamped, self-addressed return envelope with your request for information.

Be persistent. Many professionals know very little about biofeedback training yet, and some may be negative because of their lack of exposure to it. But keep asking and you'll eventually find some leads.

QUALIFICATIONS

The Biofeedback Society of America is developing a national certification board and is also encouraging state societies to work with state legislators to organize state boards to certify or license biofeedback practitioners, just as state boards license physicians, lawyers, and social workers. Progress is being made. However, the whole field is so new that biofeedback societies are just now being formed in some states. Most states still do not have licensing boards, so you will probably have to use other criteria in selecting a biofeedback trainer.

There is no agreed-upon checklist to use for verifying the qualifications of a prospective trainer. But we can offer some guidelines to consider as you look for a trainer.

Has the trainer *trained himself on instruments?* We believe that all biofeedback trainers should have trained themselves extensively before using the instruments with others. Otherwise, they are not qualified to really know what is being experienced by the people they are training. As you talk about your experience during training, the trainer should be able to help you put into words what you are experiencing because he has been there before.

A former president of the Biofeedback Society of America, Elmer Green, goes further:

> We feel that unless researchers include themselves in pilot research they really are not qualified to make many comments on the state of

consciousness, or body control, experienced by their subjects. This is not our opinion alone. That many if not most of the members of the Biofeedback Society of America agree, is a good indication that biological and psychological scientists are moving toward the existential evaluation of research findings in appropriate cases.[1]

Does the trainer *exhibit qualities of self-regulation?* The trainer should be a good advertisement for biofeedback training. He or she should be a calm and relaxed person who appears to be using the skills learned from training with the instruments. As you talk about your training experiences, the trainer can help you find ways of applying what you are learning from his own personal experiences, as well as from those of other trainees.

Is the trainer *certified or licensed?* Check to see if the trainer is certified or licensed in his or her own profession. Although most states do not certify or license biofeedback professionals, most do have some form of licensing for persons in the major helping professions—psychiatry, psychology, nursing, social work, physical therapy, and occupational therapy.

In many instances, the person actually doing the training may be called a biofeedback technician, who, although not licensed, was trained by a licensed professional and works directly for him or her. This is a common arrangement and is acceptable. Sometimes it actually is an advantage, because the technician is not distracted by other duties and responsibilities and can give you full attention.

Has the trainer *had supervised training?* At this time, there are few formal programs in colleges and universities for training biofeedback professionals. However, there are growing numbers of courses on biofeedback at both the undergraduate and graduate level, and numerous workshops offered by organizations and groups with experiences in biofeedback. (For the names of institutions or agencies offering programs, courses, or workshops, contact the Biofeedback Society of America.) Your biofeedback trainer may well have attended some of these, or made arrangements to be supervised by an experienced biofeedback trainer while learning.

Does the trainer *promise instant cures?* If so, be cautious. Biofeedback training cannot do everything, so be wary of anyone who promises you the moon. Such promises may indicate that the person is inexperienced in the field.

Do you have *confidence in the trainer?* Your reaction to the trainer seems to be important in biofeedback training just as it is when you are being treated by a physician. Feeling comfortable with and believing in the trainer will promote success in the training, so if you do have a choice, pick the trainer in whom you have the most faith.

Does the trainer *have other skills that could augment the self-regulation skills you will learn?* (Or does the trainer work with someone who does?) Among such useful skills are those used in assertiveness training, or in training to change one's environment, or to change diet or exercise patterns.

SOME CAUTIONS

There are some limitations to biofeedback training—medical, technological, and psychological—that you should know about. Here we shall list the main things you should be cautious about when you are seeking training.

Medical Considerations

When seeking help for medical problems, you should be referred to biofeedback training by your physician. Collaboration between your trainer and your doctor is advisable for a number of reasons. One reason is to ensure a correct diagnosis, so that some underlying organic problem does not go undetected. For example, your biofeedback trainer and you would want to be sure whether you have migraine headaches or pain caused by some undiagnosed irregularity or pathology in your body. Also, the doctor will need to keep tabs on your medication levels. With training, the need for medication may vary (it usually goes down), so he may need to readjust drug levels. A diabetic, for example, may need less insulin as he or she begins to apply biofeedback training skills to everyday life.

Finally, there are a few physiological situations where biofeedback training should be approached with caution. For example, someone with a long history of hypertension may have thickened and nonelastic arteries that need extra pressure for blood to circulate through them to all parts of the body. ST training for warmer hands (more relaxation), or EMG training to lower tension levels, could have negative effects by lowering blood pressure to levels not adequate to pump blood through the system.

Inaccurate Instruments

The technology of biofeedback instruments is considerably advanced, and has produced quite accurate and reliable instruments for the biofeedback professional. However, it is still possible for individuals to get kits to make their own instruments, and these are not of the same quality as those used by the biofeedback trainer.

Inaccurate instruments give inaccurate feedback. The classic example is the person who comes to a biofeedback laboratory and claims to be able to produce a great deal of theta brain waves. When attached to an EEG, he starts blinking his eyes rapidly—but no theta results. This person probably has been training on a cheap EEG biofeedback instrument. Eye blinks and eye movements can appear erroneously as brain waves in poorly constructed instruments; good EEG instruments have "artifact removers" built in to filter out such false feedback.

Psychological Considerations

As is true for those with medical disorders, individuals receiving psychotherapy should consult with their therapist before undertaking biofeedback training.

Achieving a deeply relaxed state is sometimes accompanied by strange-seeming experiences. Some persons feel as if they are tumbling through space, or can't tell where their hands or feet are with their eyes closed, or experience a feeling of weightlessness. Sometimes there is a floating sensation, or hands and feet feel as if they change size. Others may experience some nausea. These all are signs of success in relaxation. As the body changes to less activation, these sensations are common. However, they often come as a surprise to the trainee.

In persons who have had extended practice, especially in achieving very high skin temperature, very low forehead EMG levels, and EEG training toward theta, imagery may appear spontaneously. Often this is visual, ranging from colors, or flashes through scenes, or extended scenarios. Occasionally the trainee may hear sounds, or have touch or taste sensations. Such sensations are called *hypnogogic-like imagery* and are normal with this form of training. This imagery can be very useful in learning to become more deeply aware of the internal self.

These are the sorts of experiences a biofeedback trainer is trained to be aware of, so you can feel secure in letting the trainer guide you through them. Persist in your training, and make it a happy and interesting excursion into learning more about yourself.

Notes

1 E. and A. Green, *Beyond Biofeedback* (New York: Delacorte, 1977), p. 29.

BIOFEEDBACK
TRAINING
IN EDUCATION

Currently, most biofeedback training is undertaken to help adults relieve their stress-related disorders—usually disorders resulting from many years of using inappropriate responses to the tensions of daily life. But waiting to treat stress-linked problems until *after* they appear is inefficient for two reasons. One, the person has already suffered the disruption and expense of ill health. Two, it is difficult to learn new reactions and substitute them for old ones that have become nearly automatic through thousands of repetitions over many years. Wouldn't *prevention* of stress-related disorders be much better?

Effective prevention may best be accomplished by teaching *children* to manage stress. The incorporation of biofeedback training in the education of youth is just beginning to be recognized for its enormous potential. It is a topic that is under growing discussion and research in the Biofeedback Society of America.

There are many obvious payoffs for managing stress before it results in disorder or disease. For many individuals, the misery of stress disorders might be avoided altogether. For others, there would be less loss of work time, less financial cost in treating disorders, and perhaps a financial break on both medical bills and insurance premiums.

Another payoff of biofeedback training in education is *development*, which enhances the functioning of normal, healthy individuals by nurturing skills that can help them meet and exceed the normal demands and expectations of their environment.

We should repeat here that educational applications are among the newer uses of biofeedback. The three areas thought to have the most potential—prevention, development, and remediation (correcting problems when they first appear)—have had only limited research to date, and much more is needed. What has been done, however, generally shows promise, and we would like to describe some of it here.

REMEDIATION

Reading Problems

Subvocalization is the tendency to use the muscles involved in speech while reading silently. Subvocalizing severely limits silent reading speed—usually to about the rate of oral reading, 150 to 200 words per minute—not a good speed when there's lots of studying to do! Some subvocalizers whisper to themselves when reading or move their lips or jaw slightly. When just the vocal muscles are involved, individuals often are not even aware of the subvocal activity.

Students need to learn to stop subvocalizing before they can be given effective instruction to increase their reading rates. One way this can be done is to assign material with a lower reading difficulty. But this becomes impractical in high school and college. Other procedures employed to stop subvocalization are not always effective. These include holding a pencil or a handkerchief between the teeth when reading, stuffing the mouth with gum, or having someone constantly remind the subvocalizer to stop. If biofeedback training offered a quicker and more effective procedure for stopping the subvocalization, then students could get on to improving their reading speed.

One of the first reported educational uses of biofeedback training was with college students who were subvocalizers.[1] EMG feedback from the muscles on each side of the Adam's apple was used. The researchers had planned on several sessions of training but the students learned how to stop their subvocalization in one session. They continued to show the same control three months later.

High school students (grades 8 through 12) with average or above average IQs had the same results as the college students: they learned to stop subvocal speech in one session and had retained the ability when retested three months later. Students with below average IQ scores took longer to learn and were more likely to return to their subvocalization when tested later.

The researchers speculated that reading speed would increase once subvocalization was stopped, but they were unable to get the college students into a reading class to verify this. They did find that the high school students who were of above average ability and who learned to stop subvocalization did show increased reading speed when tested routinely six months later.

Sixth-grade subvocalizers were given EMG feedback training to stop lip and chin muscle activity during silent reading.[2] Again, the training helped the students effectively stop subvocal movement. This study also suggested that comprehension might increase as a result.

Speech Anxiety

Were it possible to get a show of hands from readers of this book who get anxious when talking in front of a group of people, most would have a hand in the air. This is a common fear that many of us never overcome. And it, too, has been treated by biofeedback training.

Thirty-six college students, all very much afraid of speaking before a group, demonstrated the value of heart rate feedback training to overcome their fear.[3] When first wired up to heart rate monitors, they were informed that they would have just five minutes to prepare a three-minute speech on an assigned topic. At the end of the five minutes, they had to give their speech while being rated and recorded by two deadpan observers. Heart rate and skin conductance were recorded throughout.

After this first exercise, half of the students were given two training sessions for slowing down heart rate; the other half—the control group— were given a "tracking task" of watching moving lights and pressing a switch when certain light patterns appeared. After the second training session, the students were told to give two three-minute speeches. They had five minutes to prepare each. While preparing and giving these speeches, the group that had received heart rate biofeedback training had significantly slower heart-beats as recorded on an electrocardiograph. Also, this group reported lower anxiety and was rated as showing fewer signs of anxiety by two observers who were unaware of which group had biofeedback training.

Test Anxiety

"I sure bombed on that exam," is a statement all too often uttered by students. Anxiety while taking tests and "blocking" on the answers (not being able to recall previously learned information) is common. After leaving the test room, these students can often tell you the answers they couldn't remember when taking the test. Most of us have experienced similar anxiety in some situation where we felt on the spot.

Several adults returning to school for their high school diplomas were divided into three groups. One group had EMG training, a second ST training, and a third practiced progressive relaxation (tense-relax exercises for muscles, not a true biofeedback procedure.)[4] In two of the sessions they practiced using the training while imagining things that provoked anxiety. Scores on a test-anxiety questionnaire went down only for the two biofeedback groups. Scores on a mental ability test went up when all three groups retook a comparable form of the same test after training.

It may be useful to combine practice on tests with biofeedback training for significant improvement with test-anxious students. A recent study showed that EMG training combined with practice tests resulted in superior performance when compared with EMG training alone and with practice tests alone.[5]

Students in the biofeedback training programs in the Counseling Center at Kansas State University frequently report that their training has helped them stay more relaxed while taking tests. For example, one student reported arriving for his chemistry test three or four minutes early. Instead of standing outside nervously pacing, as he usually did, he went inside, sat down and practiced what he had learned in his biofeedback training. He found he did much better on the test than on previous ones in this course. Biofeedback trainers at other schools say that they receive the same reports from their students. Biofeedback training and relaxation training, separately or together, help overcome test anxiety.

Hyperactivity

In Chapter 5 we talked about EEG biofeedback training to alleviate hyperactivity—a pattern of behavior including overactivity, impulsiveness, a very short attention span, and easily frustrated and distracted behavior. Perhaps 4 to 8 percent of all school children are hyperactive, with boys far more likely to be than girls, as are almost 40 percent of the children referred to mental health clinics.[6]

Different approaches have been used to help hyperactive children. In one study, half of a group of thirty such children had EMG feedback training of forehead muscles, and the other half had progressive relaxation training.[7] Each group had twelve training sessions, two per week for six weeks. Each session was about thirty minutes long. Parents were taught how to help their child practice a particular self-control technique at home and in stressful situations. When compared with children not having training, both the children receiving EMG biofeedback and those who learned relaxation exercises showed significant reductions in muscle-tension levels, and had improved scores on tests related to hyperactivity and in behavior ratings. The researchers concluded that EMG training would be even more helpful by doubling the training time to ten to twelve weeks, by doing more to help parent and child devise ways of using the training in specific situations at home, and by including the parents in biofeedback training so they could be more relaxed, too.

Another approach uses ST training first, to quiet the autonomic nervous system, then uses EMG training to quiet large muscle activity, and then uses EEG training to improve selective attention and decrease distractibility. Finally the child is helped to learn how to generalize this training outside the laboratory. This model has helped five of five hyperactive children ages five to nine to eliminate the need for medication and to reduce their overactivity, short attention span, and restlessness.[8]

Learning Disabilities

The potential of biofeedback for alleviating a wide variety of learning disabilities is just beginning to be explored. One form of learning disability, hyperactivity, has already been discussed. Other disabilities show promise of responding positively to biofeedback.

In one study, seventh to twelfth grade students were identified as "learning-disabled" by state-mandated criteria from scores on tests of mental ability, achievement, and personality, as well as interviews and special diagnostic tests. They were assigned to special resource rooms in their schools. Five students took training with EEG to slow their average brain wave frequencies by increasing the amount of alpha, and five were trained to speed up average frequencies by increasing the amount of beta.[9] The alpha-trained group showed significant improvement on arithmetic achievement test scores and grades in mathematics.

One sixteen-year-old learning-disabled student had a thirty-point difference between his verbal and nonverbal IQ scores, the nonverbal score being lower.[10] This suggested the possibility of some dysfunction in the right hemisphere of his brain, which "controls" nonverbal learning. This student had thirty-five sessions with EEG biofeedback training. The goal of the training was to decrease the frequency in the right hemisphere, which averaged four cycles per second faster than the left. At the end of training one month later, his right hemisphere average frequency was nine (originally fourteen), with the left staying between nine and eleven. His grades improved from a C average to an A average between his sophomore and his junior year in high school and he was making a 3.8 average (A = 4) six months later. His nonverbal IQ improved, and his parents felt that he was much less forgetful and had more "presence of mind."

When individuals are the focus of special attention (as in thirty-five training sessions and all the related contact), they often show changes just because of the attention, rather than because of the training or environmental improvements. Because of this so-called Hawthorne effect, it is difficult to say how much of this boy's improvement resulted from the EEG training and how much from being the focus of special attention. However, both the physiological and the academic changes were dramatic, suggesting promise for biofeedback training with this type of learning disability.

A group of nine elementary and middle school children in special education had twenty-three counseling sessions for forty-five minutes each. Fifteen minutes of each session was given to EMG and relaxation training. Both students and teachers reported positive effects concerning self-concept, expressing feelings, listening to others, controlling anger, getting along with others, and general classroom behavior.[11]

Some of the most dramatic effects have been found in a series of four different studies by two Texas educators.[12] The protocol for the studies was developed in a pilot investigation with four learning-disabled boys. The second study was of thirty learning-disabled elementary-age boys, divided between experimental and control groups. The third study was of sixteen educable retarded boys, eight experimental subjects and eight controls. The final study was of thirty-five "nondiagnosed" elementary boys and girls— children who were having learning problems but did not fit into any special category so were receiving no special help.

The children would meet in small groups and listen to ten minutes of a relaxation tape. Then they would practice handwriting exercises. While the group was doing the exercises, one student at a time was taken to another room and given ten minutes of EMG feedback training from the forearm. This was done three times a week for four weeks. When compared with similar children not receiving the training, these children showed significant improvements on tests of silent reading, spelling, intelligence, oral reading, auditory memory, and on a test for learning impairment.

Stuttering

The possible use of biofeedback training to alleviate stuttering was suggested to one of the authors in the early 1970s when one of the students in a Kansas State University biofeedback program reported that his regular ST and EMG training, augmented with home practice in relaxing, helped him speak up in class and in other stress situations with much less stuttering. As yet, however, there has not been much widespread research in this area. As a recent survey concluded: "The possibility of using biofeedback to modify stuttering does not yet appear to have attracted much attention. In addition, the most effective methods for treatment have not been fully researched."[13]

The "most effective methods" so far appear to be those of Lanyon, Barrington, and Newman, who used EMG feedback of the masseter muscles (a large muscle at the angle of the lower jaw that raises the jaw).[14] Eight subjects took part in ten to eighteen training sessions. All learned significant muscle relaxation in the laboratory; stuttering was greatly reduced or absent in the lab and some generalization outside the lab occurred after feedback was removed.

In another study, three stutterers in their mid-twenties practiced EMG feedback from four sites—forehead, upper lip, under the chin, and from the larynx.[15] They practiced relaxing before reading sentences tailored to include sounds which each especially stumbled over when reading. Stuttering was judged using videotape. The greatest decrease in one subject's stuttering was associated with feedback training from the lip. For the second subject, a decrease was linked to feedback from the laryngeal muscles. Decrease for the third subject seemed to be equally associated with feedback from both these sites.

PREVENTION AND DEVELOPMENT

Biofeedback training may have great potential for the *prevention* of heart attacks, high blood pressure, ulcers, insomnia, and many other stress-related disorders. Training young people to develop effective stress-coping skills early in life can have untold personal, social, and economic benefits. Such training is not as exciting to read about as the remedial work we have been describing above. It's not very dramatic to announce to a child, "Well, now that you've trained and learned better stress management, you're much less likely to have a heart attack thirty years from now!"

Biofeedback training for *development*, by which we mean training to improve performance, offers contradictory outcomes. Hundreds of individuals participating in biofeedback programs have reported that they can read faster, are more alert, have more self-confidence, or make better decisions after training. Yet, when tested systematically in laboratory studies, these results frequently are not substantiated, as reported in the next section.

Research with Armed Forces Personnel

A five-year research program supported by the Defense Department's Advanced Research Projects Agency has studied the effects on human performance of biofeedback training—especially alpha, theta, heart rate, and EMG training.[16] Would increased alpha production substitute for lack of sleep or prevent loss of performance due to lack of sleep? Would it improve memory for numbers or words, enable a person to make quicker choices, or help recuperation during short breaks in activity? The research suggested that the answers are No. However, training to suppress theta did seem to prevent or decrease drops in performance that typically occur during long periods of vigilance—three-hour radar watch periods or forty-eight hours of continuous performance on a battery of tasks. Other studies by the same agency suggest that increasing heart rate may be related to quicker and more accurate reactions and may help to prevent losses in performance due to extra stress.

Overall, however, the results of this five-year research program show that biofeedback training has only minimal effects on performance. It may be that self-control is more effective in routine daily stress situations and less powerful in very stressful situations or when doing complex tasks. Additionally, a person's intent or willfulness may be an essential ingredient in effective human performance. If additional research supports these initial studies, the conclusion may be that there is little relation between biofeedback and enhanced performance. Or, it may be that this is an area in which there are tremendous differences between individuals—for some the training helps, and for others, it doesn't. It is clear that biofeedback, like other tools, is not all things to all people and cannot always be a significant tool for improved human performance. But it would be premature to conclude that it is not beneficial to particular individuals.

Loretta Engelhardt's Biofeedback and Relaxation Skills Program

A program that emphasizes relaxation skills as a health habit, not for remediation has been developed by Loretta Engelhardt in Spearfish, South Dakota.[17] Engelhardt is a nurse and certified teacher who led the first program that offered a school-systemwide opportunity for teachers, administrators, and students to learn increased self-regulation through relaxation and biofeedback training. Since 1975, more than forty educators in Spearfish schools have participated on a voluntary basis.

Some of the teachers have adapted the program to their classrooms, from kindergarten to twelfth grade. ST and EMG readings are taken by students before and after participation in the training program, along with anxiety and self-concept tests. For twenty minutes a day, three days a week, from four to six weeks, they practice different forms of relaxation training and awareness activities, such as physical position, deep breathing, listing stress situations and stress reactions, establishing goals for the training, and keeping track of progress.

Participants are able to reduce their muscle tension levels and anxiety test-score levels as well as show increases in measures of self-concept. Students also report improvement in such aspects of their lives as athletics, attitudes, energy, and sleep. Data from this federally funded project were systematically collected for three years and analyzed by an outside researcher. The data for each of the three years consistently show the gains described. Programs such as this are preventive, because they should reduce the chances that participating students will develop the stress-related disorders so common in adults, and also developmental, because the students in them learn improved skills.

Six other school systems in South Dakota have adopted the Spearfish program, which has received approval as a model for other elementary and secondary schools. Those who elect to incorporate it can receive federal funds to help with implementation.

Norma Estrada and Student Training

An interesting program is reported by Norma Estrada, a biofeedback trainer working out of the Gladman Memorial Hospital in Oakland, California.[18] Estrada wanted to explore procedures and needs associated with introducing a biofeedback training program into a primary school setting and to get some preliminary data on the possible benefits, as reported by the pupils.

All faculty members in a private elementary school voluntarily participated in a four-month training program in biofeedback. A formal presentation to the parents resulted in an affirmative vote to incorporate the program into the regular school curriculum. All scheduling and organization was done by the students. Weekly training sessions of twenty minutes on ST and EMG biofeedback instruments were supervised by two carefully selected and trained students. Students told of using their biofeedback training during library time to improve concentration, to reduce headaches, to ready themselves for tests, and to quiet their minds during art classes, enabling more creative ideas and feelings to flow. The students are so enthusiastic, in fact, that they have volunteered to go to other schools to help start similar programs. Estrada's research is still in progress, so a final report on the program has not yet been published.

Counseling Center, Kansas State University

The first programs in biofeedback training offered regularly to large numbers of students were developed in the Counseling Center at Kansas State University by David Danskin.[19] The programs have focused primarily on prevention and development, and they generally consist of several units, each two or three weeks long.

The first unit is practice in relaxation, using the small cardboard thermometers mentioned in Chapter 3. Participants (up to sixteen in each group) learn six different relaxation exercises. They also practice on their own, keep their own daily records, and have as a goal being able to relax in a matter of seconds, anytime they wish. The second unit consists of training with either ST or EMG biofeedback instruments (participants choose which one), three times per week, usually in groups of four to six persons. The third unit is spent with the other instrument, so both skills are learned. EEG training is the last unit.

The training lab is a well-lighted, noisy room, with not-too-comfortable chairs. It is usually crowded. The lab is part of the office for two persons, who may be typing, telephoning, or talking while participants are training. In other words, the students are not isolated or insulated from the rest of the world during the training. Such conditions allow what is learned in the laboratory to become part of everyday life more readily.

After each practice session, participants discuss their training experiences with a staff member and relate them to the biofeedback. Also, they talk about their home practice (an integral part of any feedback training program), about how they are finding applications for their training, and what changes in themselves they have noted. Interestingly, the first changes often occur in unexpected ways, and we would emphasize the value of being alert to these unusual signposts—they indicate that change is beginning to take place. For example, one student in the program, a junior with an A average who joined the program out of curiosity about biofeedback, unexpectedly found himself studying 20 percent less and still getting the same grades. And we know of an artist who found that his work was changing in unexpected and usually more creative ways when all he really wanted to learn was how to work with less tension.

In this program no diagnoses are made, and no specific behavioral goals are set for the student. Rather, the focus is on practicing, applying what is practiced, and seeing when changes begin to appear. All participants keep their own records, schedule instruments, learn how to operate the instruments, and clean up. The emphasis is on self-regulation in all aspects. Naturally, participants on medication or those seeking help for physical problems are required to get the approval of their doctors before engaging in the training.

Speaking Behavior

Research on speaking behavior helps illustrate the difference between remedial and developmental applications of biofeedback training. A remedial approach would be heart rate feedback training to help *overcome fear* of speaking before a group. A developmental application would be ST training to *improve* existing speaking behavior. The study discussed in Chapter 3, in which ST-trained students were superior to nontrained students when called on to give impromptu speeches, is just one study with a developmental focus. More studies and additional research are needed, but this one does suggest the potential value of relaxation training in speech courses.

Biofeedback and Computer-Assisted Instruction

The educational potential of biofeedback instruments and teaching machines was first discussed in 1968.[20] Brain waves are an indication of how alert and attentive a student is. The combined use of an EEG instrument and a teaching machine, such as a computer, could help the student learn how to maintain an alert and attentive attitude. Also, the computer would present the material to be learned at a rate appropriate for the individual student, resulting in more efficient learning. Such computer-assisted instruction would be highly responsive both to individual differences in learning rates and variations in those individual rates.

Learning and Recall

Over the past twenty-five years, electrophysiology studies of animals and humans have suggested relationships between different brain wave patterns and learning or trying to recall previously learned material. The results of biofeedback research tend to support these studies: when individuals are focusing outside themselves and are externally alert, more beta is present in the EEG.

A possible relationship between alpha production and memory was suggested as part of a larger study.[21] Included was feedback training from three modalities—ST from the middle finger of the dominant hand, EMG from the right forearm, and alpha feedback from the left occipital region of the brain. The eighteen college males in the study were asked to read three selections, without being told why. A week later they were asked to recall those selections. There was a positive correlation between the amount of alpha produced with eyes open and recall—those who had learned to increase alpha production while speaking and with eyes open recalled the most details from the articles. Closing the eyes increases the amount of alpha in most people and opening the eyes tends to block alpha production. Could it be that eyes open alpha training could help overcome mental blocks during examinations? Research in this area certainly seems warranted.

Children, Parents, and Self-Regulation

How do children and their parents compare on the ability to control themselves? Thirty-eight pairs, each consisting of one child (six to ten years old) and one parent, were compared on the ability to control skin temperature. The children were significantly superior to their parents in the ability to voluntarily regulate their own skin temperature. The authors of the study comment:

> It seems almost ironic that children are commonly viewed by their parents and teachers as so lacking in self-control that major efforts must be made by adults to enhance this supposedly deficient characteristic. We are concerned that the actual effects of such child-rearing may be quite to the contrary and may amount to . . . 'damming up the flood of human potentialities,' changing torrents to trickles. Continued biofeedback research in children should help reveal their full neuropsychological potential.[22]

Children have the ability to regulate their minds and bodies much more easily than most adults. It seems immensely inefficient to allow children to grow up and lose the ability to self-regulate instead of helping them learn to retain these skills. Acting on this belief, one of the authors offers a course in stress management for teachers, counselors, and administrators so they can learn to integrate self-regulating, stress-managing skills into the daily school schedule.

BIOFEEDBACK IN EDUCATION

An individual's educational development results from the interplay of many forces. Although school is only one factor, it is the most structured of all such forces. To increase the active role of the student in the schooling process, what could be more appropriate than to include in the regular curriculum a course of study designed to place the power for self-development in the hands of each individual student?

Biofeedback offers such an approach. Learning voluntary control of single bodily processes (such as muscle tension) could perhaps begin in elementary school. It could progress through experience in learning to control multiple processes. Understanding the concommitant psychological states and their voluntary self-regulation could follow.

With this inner knowledge, students would be able to learn how to "shift" themselves into the psychophysiological state most appropriate for each learning task at hand. For example, they could learn to achieve voluntarily the state of attention most conducive to learning new material; could shift easily to the state associated with nonanxious, efficient recall while taking tests; and could alter their state yet again for performing physical activities.

Such a course would open up a whole new area of study for each student: "inner space," the world within each individual. Biofeedback is demonstrating that from inner space comes creative, intuitive knowledge and insights. When integrated with the cognitive knowledge emphasized in our schools and colleges, such inner knowledge might add dimensions that previously have been limited mostly to philosophical and theoretical contemplation.

Biofeedback training puts the power to alter one's own behavior in the hands of the individual. It stands in sharp contrast to current methods of behavior training, which often rely on mood-changing drugs to control the behavior of hundreds of thousands of American school children, or use mechanistic systematic conditioning of behavior and other *external* agents or authorities. Of all behavior modification techniques, biofeedback is the first to rely on each individual's ability to guide his own destiny.[23]

Notes

1 C. D. Hardyck, L. F. Petrinovich, and D. W. Ellsworth, "Feedback of Speech Muscle Activity during Silent Reading: Rapid Extinction," *Science,* 1966, Vol. 154, pp. 1467–1468. Also appears in T. Barber and others, eds., *Biofeedback and Self-Control* (Chicago: Aldine-Atherton, 1971). See also C. D. Hardyck and L. F. Petrinovich, "Treatment of Subvocal Speech during Reading," *Journal of Reading,* 1969, Vol. 12, pp. 361–422.

2 L. Parsky and J. D. Papsdorf, "EMG Biofeedback Suppression of Subvocalization in Reading Disabled Grade VI Students," *Proceedings of the Biofeedback Research Society, 1976* (Denver: Biofeedback Research Society, 1976).

3 R. J. Gatchel and J. D. Proctor, "Effectiveness of Voluntary Heart Rate Control in Reducing Speech Anxiety," *Journal of Consulting and Clinical Psychology,* 1976, Vol.

44, pp. 381–389, and in J. Kamiya and others, eds., *Biofeedback and Self-Control, 1976–77* (Chicago: Aldine, 1977).

4 J. R. Bernthal and J. D. Papsdorf, "The Effects of Different Forms of Relaxation Training on Text Anxiety and Test Performance," *Proceedings of the Biofeedback Society of America, 1977* (Denver: Biofeedback Society of America, 1977).

5 G. K. Hodge and F. A. Collatz, "Efficacy of EMG Biofeedback Training in Improving Examination Performance of Test Anxious College Students," *Proceedings of the Biofeedback Society of America, 1980.*

6 L. W. Braud, "The Effects of Frontal EMG Biofeedback and Progressive Relaxation upon Hyperactivity and its Behavioral Concomitants," *Biofeedback and Self-Regulation, 1978*, Vol. 3, pp. 69–89.

7 *Ibid.*

8 N. Estrada, "Biofeedback and Hyperactivity: A Case Study," in M. J. Fine, ed., *Case Studies in Hyperactivity* (Jamaica, NY: Spectrum Publishers, 1978). Also N. Estrada and A. E. Gladman, "Biofeedback and the Hyperactive Child," mimeographed, Everett Gladman Memorial Hospital, Oakland, CA, 1977.

9 P. J. Murphy, J. Darwin, and D. A. Murphy, "EEG Feedback Training or Cerebral Dysfunction: A Research Program with Learning Disabled Adolescents," *Proceedings of the Biofeedback Society of America, 1977.*

10 *Ibid.*

11 F. Mayo, "EMG/Relaxation Training—Counseling Elementary and Middle School Students in Special Education," *Proceedings of the Biofeedback Society of America, 1980.*

12 H. L. Russel and J. L. Carter, "Academic Gains in Learning Disabled Children after Biofeedback/Relaxation Training," *Proceedings of the Biofeedback Society of America, 1979.*

13 S. M. Davis and C. E. Drichta "Biofeedback Theory and Application in Allied Health: Speech Pathology," *Biofeedback and Self-Regulation, 1980*, Vol. 5, p. 166.

14 R. I. Lanyon, C. C. Barrington, and A. C. Newman, "Modification of Stuttering through EMG Biofeedback: A Preliminary Study," *Behavior Therapy, 1976*, Vol. 7, pp. 96–103.

15 B. Guitar, "Reduction of Stuttering Frequency using Analogue Electromyograph Feedback," *Journal of Speech and Hearing Research, 1975*, Vol. 18, pp. 672–685.

16 G. H. Lawrence and L. C. Johnson, "Biofeedback and Performance," chapter in G. Schwartz and J. Beatty, eds., *Biofeedback: Theory and Research* (Academic Press, 1977).

17 L. Engelhardt, "The Application of Biofeedback Techniques with a Public School Setting," *Proceedings of the Biofeedback Society of America, 1976 and 1978.*

18 N. Estrada, "Biofeedback Training Used to Enhance Biological Awareness in a Private School Setting," paper prepared for Union Graduate School West. Estrada's address is given in note 8.

19 For the most detailed description of these programs, see the tape by D. G. Danskin and T. J. Lowenstein, "Biofeedback Applications in Counseling and Education," BioMonitoring Applications, Inc., 270 Madison, New York 10016, 1977. This is a 60-minute cassette tape, part of BMA's cassette series on biofeedback.

20 T. Mulholland, "Feedback Encephalograph," *Activitas Nervosa Superior*, 1968, Vol. 10, No. 4. Reprinted in T. Barber, and others, eds., *Biofeedback and Self-Control* (1971).

21 E. Green, "Biofeedback for Mind-Body Self-Regulation: Healing and Creativity," in D. Shapiro and others, eds., *Biofeedback and Self-Control, 1972*, (Chicago: Aldine, 1973).

22 G. Loughry-Machado and S. Suter, "Skin Temperature Biofeedback in Children and Their Parents," *Proceedings of the Biofeedback Society of America, 1979*.

23 D. G. Danskin and E. D. Walters, "Biofeedback and Voluntary Self-Regulation: Counseling and Education," *Personnel and Guidance Journal*, 1973, Vol. 51, pp. 633–638.

RELAXATION
TECHNIQUES

As we stated in the first chapter, the critical step in biofeedback is "training"—practicing with the information fed back—in order to achieve voluntary self-regulation, which is the ultimate goal of the whole process. Should you participate in biofeedback training, as part of your training your trainer will probably teach you one or several relaxation techniques. This chapter introduces a number of them.

These exercises, in combination with monitoring the resulting changes fed back by the biofeedback instrument, help the individual develop increased awareness and sensitivity to the internal sensations that accompany changes in physiological and emotional states. All of us are capable of detecting gross changes in our own physiological or emotional states (large changes in heart rate, muscle tension, mood swings). Few people seem capable, without conscious training, of detecting small changes in these same states. Yet it is these small changes, building slowly throughout the day, that eventually can lead to stress reactions such as headaches, ulcers, insomnia, hypertension, or any of the disorders we have mentioned throughout this book.

People sometimes complain, "That headache hit me all at once, from out of nowhere!" While this may seem true, the headache actually has been building up over a period of time. An individual must first learn to note the small physiological changes which eventually bring on the headache. This increased awareness, coupled with the skill of increased self-regulation learned from biofeedback, can be used to control these changes, which thereby enables the person to control the headache.

Relaxation techniques can help increase the initial awareness required. They can also suggest some training strategies, and can be valuable in learning how to relax voluntarily any time, any place.

We have alluded to several different relaxation techniques while discussing the various biofeedback instruments. We have also given examples of short exercises that a person can use. We will now present in greater detail examples of relaxation exercises that your biofeedback trainer might use with you. These exercises can be of great benefit when practiced daily. For many individuals, combining such exercises with regular biofeedback training seems to facilitate greatly the growth-of-awareness process associated with voluntary control. In time, the use of machines might be eliminated altogether.

When and where should these techniques be practiced? The first few times, you will probably prefer a quiet place, with outside pressures and distractions minimized. Your biofeedback trainer may recommend that as you become more adept at the techniques you should try to do them anywhere. At this point, you should welcome distractions while practicing, because they provide practice under the circumstances in which you want more voluntary control. After all, one of the major goals is to be able to voluntarily regulate our mind, body, and emotions throughout the day, under all conditions. But, to begin, find a comfortable, quiet place.

Your trainer may have you practice exercises while lying down or sitting. Just don't go to sleep—you can't learn much about voluntary self-regulation while sleeping. Eventually, though, you will learn to do the exercises in many positions and circumstances.

How frequently should you practice? As with most skills, the more you practice the quicker you will learn and the more proficient you will become. Initially, your exercises may take thirty minutes. As you become more proficient, you'll find that you can achieve equal degrees of control in less and less time.

TENSE-RELAX

One of the most frequently used techniques is the tense-relax exercise, an abbreviated variation of a training program called progressive relaxation.[1] To learn effective differential control of muscles takes up to a year. The exercise you'll learn can be mastered in a much shorter time. Its purpose is to help you learn awareness and control of very small changes in muscle tension levels.

To begin the tense-relax exercise, find a comfortable position. Very gently close your eyes. (A small percentage of people prefer to have their eyes open.) Take a deep breath, hold it for the count of four, and then exhale slowly, letting all tension fade away as your body begins to relax. Breathe normally with your eyes still closed. Scan your body for any signs of tension. Notice any tightness, pressure, or pain anywhere in your body. At first, this may take a minute or two, but with practice you will become aware of your tension level in just a few seconds. Then, scan to identify those areas where you already are quite relaxed.

Begin by clenching your fists (let your arms rest in your lap or at your sides). Hold them clenched for about five seconds, while letting the other muscles in your body remain relaxed. Notice where the tension is and how it feels. Then relax. Let go all at once, don't ease off. Now, be aware of how the muscles feel as they let go and relax more and more. This letting-go feeling is what you are most interested in—it is what's associated with relaxation and what you can learn to do more and more.

Now, pull your forearms up against your upper arms and feel the tension in your biceps. Hold that for five seconds or so. Then let go all at once and "tune in" those feelings of relaxation.

Tighten your forehead muscles as much as you can. Hold for five seconds, noting how it feels. (Let those other muscles in your body remain relaxed.) Notice where the central focus of tension is and the adjacent muscles that are affected just by tightening the forehead. Now, release that tension and pay close attention to how the muscles feel at the various levels as they drift toward relaxation. After having been tight, the muscles let go by stages. It is these stages that you will learn to recognize and become familiar with. Once you can identify the various degrees of muscle tension-relaxation, you can duplicate any level you desire. Most people can duplicate the tense levels at will; it is the relaxed levels that are more difficult and that are learned through this exercise.

Now, close your eyes tightly. Hold for five seconds. Then, let go and be aware of the feeling as the muscles relax more and more.

With your eyes closed, roll your eyes in a large circle. *Be careful;* these muscles can be strained, so make the circles just large enough so you can feel the wave of tension go round and round. Then relax.

Using the same process of tensing and relaxing, go through the following: clench your jaws; move your tongue up and down, left, right; tense your neck muscles by first tensing the muscles that move your head back, and while holding these tense, tensing those that move your head forward, to the right, and then to the left; try to touch your shoulders in front of you; try to touch your shoulder blades together. Continue through the rest of your body—abdomen, thighs, calves, feet. Each time, tense and then let go and be aware of the muscles as they relax more and more.

Once you have completed tensing and relaxing all muscles in the body, again take a deep breath, hold it for the count of four and release it slowly. At this point notice once again how your entire body feels. See if any tension that you may have noticed prior to the exercise is still present. When you decide to end the exercise, stretch fully and then continue with your daily activity. By practicing this exercise, you can learn to recognize tension when it first begins to build (any slight change in muscle tension can be noticed), and at that time reduce it to a comfortable level.

AUTOGENIC TRAINING

Another technique often used in conjunction with biofeedback training is taken from a system called Autogenic Training.[2] As we mentioned earlier in the book, the Greens of the Menninger Foundation have developed a version of Autogenic Training that has been used in biofeedback centers across the nation.[3]

Again, find a comfortable position, close your eyes, and take a deep breath. Hold it, then exhale slowly. Notice your tension level for a few seconds. Check out those areas where you feel tense. Then check those that are most relaxed. Once you have completed this, try to let your mind go blank. Try to concentrate on absolutely nothing for fifteen seconds (a very difficult thing to do for most of us). Then slowly begin repeating to yourself the phrases suggested by your trainer, such as "I am very quiet." Go over the phrase in your mind three or four times. Some people coordinate this with their breathing. Inhale normally, and as you begin to exhale, at the top of your breathing cycle, slowly repeat the phrase. Try to feel as calm as you can while you repeat the phrase to yourself. Let the tension soar away as you feel yourself drift toward deeper states of relaxation.

Next, focus on your feet and feel heaviness and warmth in them (heaviness and warmth are associated with relaxation). You might mentally repeat three or four times, "My feet are heavy and warm." Then feel the ankles, legs, and hips as heavy and warm, and mentally repeat "My ankles, legs, and hips are heavy and warm." Continue through the rest of the body this way. When you get to your head, associate smooth muscles with relaxation, and imagine the muscles in your forehead lengthening and smoothing out.

After you have gone through the legs, torso, and head this way, focus on your arms and hands. Repeat such phrases (and feel them happening) as "My hands are warm," or "My hands are warm, relaxed and warm," or "I can feel the warmth flowing down my arms into my hands." Recall from Chapter 3 that warmth in the hands accompanies relaxation for many people— warmth is felt when the blood vessels in the fingers dilate and more blood flows into the hands.

Then, you might repeat a series of phrases about calm and quiet thoughts, abou focusing internally and feeling at peace.

As you repeat these phrases, also visualize and feel them actually happening. Visualization and feeling are important in "communicating" what we want the body to do. Let yourself go. Let the relaxation occur, don't force it. Stay with the exercise as long as you like, but when you decide to finish it, take another deep breath, hold it for a count of four and then exhale slowly. At this point notice if the tension has left those areas that were tight before you began the exercise. Then stretch and get up and continue you daily activity.

VISUALIZATION

Here is a short exercise using a type of visualization. Begin the exercise in the usual manner—close your eyes, take a deep breath, and check out your initial body tension and relaxation. Then, concentrate on your forehead. In your mind, try to visualize the forehead muscles. Study your forehead for any signs of tension and try to visualize it being as relaxed as possible.

You might want to visualize someone rubbing your brow, or use any other visualization device that works for you. Then, as in the tense-relax exercise, proceed through each muscle of the body—visualizing the muscle and its current tension level and then visualizing the muscle relaxing. Many people we have worked with have become very creative in the visualizations they use to relax each individual muscle. Experiment and find those visualizations that work the best for you. They may seem artificial or "corny" to you at the time— but if they achieve the desired result, that is all that matters.

SELF-DIRECTED IMAGERY

Another useful exercise that can be done at home involves self-directed imagery. Such imagery is a form of visualization. Many people prefer it because it is less structured than most relaxation exercises and allows a little more freedom for the mind. (This can be a problem for some, however; one's mind may drift to tension-producing thoughts during a nonrote type of exercise.)

Self-directed imagery involves going through a particularly pleasant scene in your mind. After beginning the exercise in the usual manner, when you begin to feel comfortable, develop a scenario in your mind. Imagine yourself on a beach, or in a forest, or skiing, or in whatever situation that is relaxing to you. It should be noted that what may be relaxing for one person may be stressful to another, so experiment until you find the right scene.

Once you have settled on a scene, make it as real as you can. Try to involve all five senses mentally. For instance, you might envision yourself at the edge of a forest. Try to make the scene as restful and lifelike as you can. Imagine the sky and the sun. Feel the warmth on your skin. Notice a small breeze and the fresh clean smell of the outdoors. Notice how the sunlight is broken up by the trees as it filters down through the branches. Listen for the birds calling back and forth, or the squirrels chattering to one another. In your mind, begin to walk into the forest at a very leisurely pace. Imagine the sound the dry leaves and twigs would make as you step down on them. As you mentally walk through the forest you may come to a small stream gently flowing through the woods. Notice how clean and clear the water is. Maybe there are small fish swimming in the sparkling water. Watch them as they dart back and forth from rock to rock on the bottom. Continue with the scene as long as you want, making it as vivid as you possibly can. If your mind should wander, bring it back to some part of your scene and continue with the exercise. When you decide to end your scene, breathe deeply, exhale slowly, stretch and then continue with your regular daily activity.

This particular exercise is a versatile one because you can keep it fresh by simply changing scenes. If you get bored with one scene, find another that is equally relaxing. Again, the exercise may seem somewhat "corny" at first, but as you realize the stress and tension reduction brought about by this simple "daydream" technique, its value becomes quite clear.

BREATHING

Here is a deceptively simple exercise that has been very helpful to many persons doing biofeedback training. The exercise is breathing evenly in and out while focusing on the tip of your nose. With your eyes closed, become gently aware of the air coming in and out of your nostrils. Perhaps you'll notice that the air coming in seems cool and the air going out seems warm. Don't frown or tighten up—just let your forehead and closed eyes remain relaxed while you become acutely aware of the air entering and leaving your nostrils. Breathe in to a count of four and out to the same count, breathing evenly. If your mind wanders, gently bring it back, concentrating on the tip of your nose.

These are just a few of the exercises your biofeedback trainer might teach you. The value of consistent practice cannot be overstated.

In addition to these specific relaxation techniques, there are many things you can do throughout the day when you do not have time to do a "formal" exercise. We have hinted at a few of these and described others throughout this book. Because of their importance, we would like to mention some of them again here.

THE WAITING GAME (MINI-EXERCISES)

One of the most common complaints (excuses) that a biofeedback trainer hears is, "I don't have time to sit down and go through these exercises." This may or may not be the case, but an individual always has some "dead time" throughout the day. Dead time is simply periods when we are caught standing, waiting, sitting, or looking with nothing to do. Waiting in bank lines, waiting for the light to turn green, waiting in restaurants, waiting in drive-through lines, waiting for the train to finish crossing, waiting for the bus or subway, waiting for the dryer to stop or the baby to wake up—these are just a few of the dozens of times during the day when we have time to kill.

These are moments when you can do a mini-exercise. Once you have learned to identify certain tension levels you can make periodic checks throughout the day and constantly reduce your tension level. Granted, there is not enough time during these odd moments to do a formal exercise, but you will be surprised how much more energy you will have at the end of the day by simply "letting go" whenever you find yourself in a waiting situation.

Unfortunately, most of the times mentioned above are used by many of us in just the opposite way. We come away from these situations more stressed instead of more relaxed. While you are waiting at the stoplight, notice the person in the car next to you. Watch him throw his arm over the back of the seat or move about nervously. The next time you are waiting in a crowd for an elevator that is slow to come, notice how many times the button gets pushed—three, four, five times. The elevator will get there when it gets there, but we are always in a hurry. We make these dead times (times we very often can do nothing about) work against us instead of for us. Why come away from these situations more tense? We already have enough times during the day when we are going to be stressed. Why add more? Make these times work for you. Relax, lower your shoulders, take a deep breath, close your eyes for a second. Just enjoy a minute to yourself. When you do, you will be surprised not only at how relaxed you are as you go through the day, but also how quickly those annoying little waits actually go by.

The above techniques are all good examples of exercises you can do to learn proper relaxation skills. The biofeedback instruments, the biofeedback training, and the consistent repetition at home and throughout the day will soon help you gain voluntary self-regulation—the ability to handle your own stress. That ability is most certainly worth the effort. Better health means better living. It's up to each of us.

Notes

1 For a description of this program, see E. Jacobson, *Self-Operations Control*, which is a manual to be used in conjunction with professional instruction. It may be obtained from the National Foundation for Progressive Relaxation, 55 E. Washington St., Suite 311, Chicago, IL 60602. A less technical version is E. Jacobson, *You Must Relax* (New York: McGraw-Hill, 1978).

2 J. H. Schultz and W. Luthe, *Autogenic Training: A Psychophysiologic Approach to Psychotherapy* (New York: Grune and Stratton, 1959; and W. Luthe, ed., *Autogenic Therapy: Volumes I-VI* (New York: Grune and Stratton, 1969).

3 E. and A. Green, *Beyond Biofeedback* (New York: Delacorte, 1977), pp. 337–338.

ADDITIONAL READING
AND LISTENING

Books

E. and A. Green. *Beyond Biofeedback.* New York: Delacorte Press, 1977 (hardback). A Delta Book, Dell Publishing Co., 1977 (paperback). A personal account of the research of two of the leaders in biofeedback. The first half of the book discusses their work in biofeedback training; the second half goes beyond biofeedback and presents broader implications. Offers an excellent explanation of how and why biofeedback works.

B. B. Brown. *Stress and the Art of Biofeedback.* New York: Harper & Row, 1977. By another pioneer in the field; discusses the ties between biofeedback and stress-induced disorders.

T. X. Barber and others, Editors. *Biofeedback and Self-Control.* Chicago: Aldine Publishing Co., 1970–. An annual, published since 1970, in which the leading articles in the field are reprinted. These are usually quite technical and written for the professional, but they offer a sample of current research.

Francine Butler. *Biofeedback: A Survey of the Literature.* New York: Plenum Press, 1978. A most complete bibliography, compiled by the Executive Director of the Biofeedback Society of America. Order from: Plenum Publishing Corporation, 227 West 17th Street, New York, NY 10011.

Abstracts

Abstracts of papers presented at the Annual Meeting of the Biofeedback Society of America are available from the office of the Society. Contact the Executive Director at the address below for prices.

Journals

Biofeedback and Self-Regulation is published four times a year and is the official journal of the Biofeedback Society of America.

Audio Cassette Tapes

Specially prepared recordings of leading biofeedback researchers and practitioners discussing many aspects of biofeedback training. The number of different tapes is approaching 100. Available from BioMonitoring Applications, Inc., 270 Madison Avenue, New York, NY 10016.

Professional Societies

Biofeedback Society of America
4301 Owens St.
Wheat Ridge, CO 80033

GLOSSARY

Alpha brain wave rhythm   One of the four major types of brain wave patterns, characterized by frequencies of 8 to 13 cycles per second in the electroencephalogram. Usually begins to appear when eyes are closed and the body is relaxing.

Autogenic training   A system of treatment especially useful with mind-body or psychosomatic problems. Uses phrases or verbal formulas, such as, "My hand is heavy and warm." Regular practice with the training exercises has helped with a wide variety of stress-related disorders.

Baseline   The measurement of the average level of physiological function taken prior to training in order to determine the degree of change of the trainee.

Beta brain wave rhythm   One of the four major types of brain wave patterns, characterized by frequencies of 13 cycles per second and higher in the electroencephalogram. Usually associated with an active mental state, such as learning or thinking about concrete problems.

Biofeedback   Information delivered (fed back) to an individual about his ongoing biological processes. Usually employs sensitive electronic instruments which detect minute changes in muscle tension, skin temperature, or brain waves, and which filter, amplify, and display these to the person.

Biofeedback training   The use of instrument feedback to learn how to make changes voluntarily in whichever physiological process is being monitored.

Crisis intervention   Entering into a person's life after he has become ill or has some emergency.

Delta brain wave rhythm   One of the four major types of brain wave patterns, characterized by frequencies of 0.5 to 4 cycles per second in the electroencephalogram. Usually appears when persons are asleep and not dreaming, or unconscious.

Desensitization   A system for helping reduce anxiety felt in specific situations. If the feared situation is speaking before a group, for example, a therapist helps the person develop a series of mental pictures. The series begins with the least frightening behavior, such as getting dressed to go give a speech, and ends with the most frightening behavior, such as actually giving the speech in front of an audience. After training to relax, the person practices staying relaxed while progressing through the series of mental pictures. In time, he desensitizes himself to anxiety in the situation and can perform more calmly.

EEG biofeedback   Abbreviation for electroencephalographic biofeedback. Detects the minute electrical signals from some location on the scalp and delivers the signal (feeds it back) by visual or auditory means. Also called brain wave feedback.

Electrode   A device used for detecting electrical potentials on the surface of the body (used with EMG, EEG, or electrocardiogram). Attached to the skin with a gelatinlike substance or tape.

Electroencephalograph   An instrument used to record the electrical activity of the brain.

Electromyograph   An instrument used to record the electrical neural activity associated with muscle action.

EMG biofeedback   Abbreviation for electromyographic biofeedback. Detects the minute electrical signals associated with contracting and relaxing muscles, and delivers the signal (feeds it back) by visual or auditory means.

Galvanic Skin Response (GSR)   A tiny electrical current conducted by the skin, which can be detected and displayed by an instrument—which is itself sometimes called a GSR.

Germ theory   The theory that illnesses are caused by the action of external agents, such as microbes or viruses, which enter the body.

Guided imagery   A form of visualization. A relaxation technique in which '
the trainee visualizes a calm, pleasant scene in the mind while trying to
incorporate all five senses into the image.

Hypertension   High blood pressure. Essential hypertension is high blood
pressure with no apparent organic cause, thus probably resulting
from stress.

Microvolt   One millionth of a volt of electrical current; a measurement used
in biofeedback.

Neuromuscular re-education   The retraining of nerves and muscles damaged by injury, stroke, or disease.

Passive volition   The term used to refer to the process of "letting it happen,"
which is involved in learning to voluntarily regulate mind and body.

Psychophysiology   Involving the mind and the body together. Refers to the
effects of the mental and emotional processes on the physiology of the
body, and the effects of the physiological processes of the body on the
mental and emotional processes.

Progressive relaxation   A muscular relaxation system developed by Ed-
mund Jacobson. It involves alternately contracting and relaxing muscle groups, progressing through the body until all groups have been
trained. Usually takes about a year to complete training.

Psychosomatic reaction   A physiological change produced by mental or
psychological stress. The change may be brief and mild, as a tension
headache or nervous stomach, or continuous and serious, as high
blood pressure or ulcers.

Response stereotypy   The theory that many people have one physiological
system which is more responsive to stress than the other systems.

Sensorimotor rhythm (SMR)   Name given to a 12 to 16 cycle per second
EEG signal detected by electrodes placed over the sensory and motor
areas of the brain located approximately above the ears toward the
top of the head.

Skin temperature feedback   Feedback that indicates changes in skin temperature. Also called thermal feedback. One of the simplest and most
frequently used forms of biofeedback.

Social Readjustment Rating Scale   A scale to measure the relative amount of
stress from particular events that occur in people's lives.

Stress   The pressure or strain exerted on a system.

Tense-relax training   A shortened form of progressive relaxation, involving
the tensing and then the relaxing of a muscle group.

Thermal feedback   Another name for skin temperature feedback.

Thermistor   A device, usually taped to the skin, used to monitor skin temperature.

Theta brain wave rhythm   One of the four major types of brain wave patterns, characterized by frequencies of 4 or 8 cycles per second in the electroencephalogram. Usually appears as a person becomes drowsy and is dropping off to sleep. Sometimes associated with "mini-dreams" or the sort of images that occur in dreams.

Visualization   A relaxation technique using mental images. For example, the individual might relax various muscles in the body by mentally seeing (visualizing) the muscle relaxing.

Voluntary self-regulation   The goal of biofeedback training; the ability to make specific bodily changes without aid of a trainer or instruments.

INDEX

Alpha rhythms. *See* Brain wave rhythms

Alpha-theta training, 60

Anxiety: control of with EMG biofeedback, 45–46, 85–86; control of with EEG biofeedback, 60–61, 63; associated with speech, 85; associated with test taking, 85–86

Asthma, 48, 73

Autogenic training, 22, 41, 101–102; stages of, 22–23; in combination with biofeedback training, 24; in reduction of migraine headaches, 24

Behavior: characteristics of type A, 15–16; link to heart disease, 15–16; in development of cancer, 16–17

Beta rhythms. *See* Brain wave rhythms

Biofeedback: defined, 2–4; role of patient with, 4; cautions in use of, 81–82

Biofeedback equipment: development of, 3; safety of, 3, 31

Biofeedback Society of America, 79, 107

Biofeedback trainer, 78, 79–80, 82; qualifications of, 79–80

Biofeedback training, 2, 3, 4; major focus of, 4; need for practice, 99

Blood pressure feedback, 71–72. *See also* Hypertension

Blood sugar level feedback, 76

Brain wave rhythms: identification of, 53-56; alpha rhythms, 53, 55, 60, 62, 63, 93, 94; beta rhythms, 53, 55, 60, 62, 93; delta rhythms, 55, 58, 59; theta rhythms, 55, 64, 82; synchronous rhythms, 65
Breathing: equalized, 27; thoracic, 73, 74; abdominal, 74; exercise used for, 103-104
Bruxism, 48

Computer-Assisted Instruction, 93
Coronary heart disease, 5, 15, 16
Crisis intervention, 7

Dead time, 104-105
Delta rhythms, *See* Brain wave rhythms
Diabetes, 76, 81
Diarrhea (functional), 73

Electroencephalographic biofeedback (EEG): defined, 52; benefits of, 53; instruments, 56; electrode placement, 56-57; goal of, 57; training sessions, 57, 58; history of, 58-61; applications, 61-65, 87; future of, 65-66
Electromyographic biofeedback (EMG): defined, 38-39; electrode placement, 39, 40; techniques used with, 41-42; applications, 42-49, 87
Engelhardt, Loretta: relaxation skills program, 90-91
Epilepsy, 53, 57, 61, 62
Estrada, Norma: programs of, 91-92

Fight-flight response, 11-13, 17-18, 19

Galvanic skin response: defined, 68; uses of, 69-70
General Adaptation Syndrome (GAS), 17-19
Germ theory, 7

Hawthorne effect, 88
Heart rate feedback, 70-71, 73
Hyperactivity, 62-63, 75, 86-87
Hyperhidrosis, 74-75
Hypertension, 5, 8, 26, 72, 81; essential, 14, 26
Hypnogogic imagery, 82

Insomnia, 28, 48, 74

Kansas State University: program for stuttering, 88–89; counseling center programs, 92–93

Learning disabilities, 87–88

Meditation: autogenic, 23; yoga, 58; zazen, 59
Menninger Foundation, 22, 25, 26, 59, 101
Menstrual cramps, 28
Migraine headaches, 6, 7, 24–25

Neuromuscular re-education, 48–49

Obsessions, 62

Passive volition, 35
Personality. *See* Behavior
Phobias, 47, 69
Premature Ventricular Contractions (PVC), 70–71, 73
Prisoner rehabilitation, 28
Progressive relaxation, 99. *See also* Tense-relax exercise
Psychosis, 47
Psychosomatic disorders, 6, 8

Respiration feedback, 73–74
Response sterotypy, 14–15

Self-directing imagery, 34, 102
Skin temperature biofeedback: defined, 22; applications, 24–27, 28–29, 87; instruments, 29–31; training sessions, 32–34; technique used with, 33–34; goals of, 33, 35; sensations associated with, 36
Social Readjustment Rating Scale, 9–11
Spastic colon, 73
Speech difficulties, 93, stuttering, 88–89
Sphincter feedback, 75
Stabilimeter feedback, 75
Stethoscope feedback, 72–73
Stomach acidity level feedback, 75
Stress, 5–6, 7, 52; cost of, 8–9; defined, 9; causes of, 11; as defined by Selye, 17
Student training, 91–92
Stuttering. *See* Speech difficulties

Subvocalization, 84–85
Swami Rama, 59, 60
Synchronous brain waves. *See* Brain wave rhythms
Systematic desensitization, 47, 69, 73

Tachycardia, 71
Tense-relax exercise, 41–42, 71, 99–101
Tension headaches, 6, 43–45
Theta rhythms. *See* Brain waves rhythms
Torticollis, 48
Twilight learning, 64–65

Ulcers, 6, 75

Vapor pressure feedback, 74–75
Visualization, 34–35, 41, 58, 102
Voluntary self-regulation, 2, 3–4, 36, 98